THE PATH UNEXPLORED
SUCCESS MANTRA OF BrahMos

THE PATH UNEXPLORED
SUCCESS MANTRA OF BrahMos

A Sivathanu Pillai

Foreword by

Dr APJ Abdul Kalam

The Path Unexplored: Success Mantra of BrahMos
A Sivathanu Pillai

First Published in 2014

ISBN 978-81-8274-803-3

Published by
PENTAGON PRESS
206, Peacock Lane, Shahpur Jat
New Delhi-110049
Phones: 011-64706243, 26491568
Telefax: 011-26490600
email: rajan@pentagonpress.in
website: www.pentagonpress.in

Branch:
Prime Arcade
Office #11
1154 Saifee Street
Opp. M.G.Road, Camp
Pune-411001
Email: pentagonpresspune@gmail.com

Printed at Aegean Offset Printers, Greater Noida (U.P)

This book is dedicated to the everlasting friendship between India and the Russian Federation, and to Team BrahMos.

Royalty accrued to the author through the sale of this book will be contributed towards the welfare of Team BrahMos.

CONTENTS

FOREWORD

Dr. A.P.J. Abdul Kalam
Former President of India

10, Rajaji Marg
New Delhi-110011

A Unique Joint Technological Venture

The Joint Venture 'BrahMos' signifies great friendship and trust between India and Russia in high technology cooperation. The best talent from both nations have been pooled together to achieve the supersonic cruise missile which has outsmarted the developed world.

I was always longing, when India will become the first Nation to possess the most advanced system in the world. BRAHMOS made India proud by making it the first Nation to have a universal operational supersonic cruise missile delivered to the Indian Armed Forces thereby demolishing the Sixth Nation Syndrome. There is no equivalent operational system elsewhere in the world to have speed, precision and power and the universality demonstrated by BRAHMOS. I also know that we started BrahMos with a mere $ 300 million investment by both countries and today the business of the company has crossed $ 6 billion. My desire is now to see the BrahMos business crossing beyond $ 10 billion and to achieve a unique status in the world, connecting the oceans and making new strategic partners beyond the borders.

It is a long story how we could make BrahMos a reality. The path-breaking formation of Joint Venture was not easy. My friend Dr. Yefremov, the then Director General of NPO Mashinostroyenia, is a unique person of respect, who got convinced after visiting the DRDO laboratories that Joint Venture is feasible. This is a unique joint venture with a ratio of 50.5:49.5 giving full empowerment to the JV Company the result of which has traversed its course from mind to market. BrahMos is a fine example of role model of courage and leadership. Different versions, continuous product improvement and integration of the user at every stage made the weapon system user-friendly. All the three wings of the Indian Armed Forces cherish BRAHMOS as their product to be deployed as a prime weapon. Thus, BrahMos is a live example of excellent leadership, system design, system engineering, system integration and system management. The results show that this successful model must be replicated in many other areas both in military and in civil as a national model.

Dr. A Sivathanu Pillai, Distinguished Scientist and Chief Controller Research & Development of DRDO and also the Founder CEO & MD of BrahMos Aerospace was my colleague for more than three decades starting from SLV-3 days to IGMDP days and beyond. He made significant contributions in the launch vehicle programme of ISRO and in realizing critical missile technologies for Guided Missile Programme of DRDO through a network of academic institutions and industries thus combating effectively the technology control regime. Dr. Pillai's great leadership in bringing out BRAHMOS from mind to market, integrating the best brains of India and Russia and multiple institutions and industries to realize this world class product is commendable. BRAHMOS missile has been inducted in the Indian Armed Forces to their complete satisfaction.

BrahMos has made a page in the history of the world and Dr. Pillai is synonymous with BrahMos. He has shared many of his interesting experiences during the process of evolution of BrahMos, in this book. I consider this book a valuable narration to the young scientists, technologists, techno-managers and the youth and experienced who aspire to excel in this competitive world. I wish the readers to emulate the role model BrahMos Joint Venture and learn from its experiences.

28 February 2014

(A.P.J. Abdul Kalam)

PROLUSION

This book is a great creative work, dedicated to history of creation, development and perspectives of the most advanced form of military-technical cooperation - Joint Russian-Indian project for creation of missile complexes of different kind of deployment with an anti ship missile (Project "BrahMos").

The value of this book lies in the fact that its author Dr. Pillai is a Distinguished Scientist and Managing Director & Chief Executive Officer of Joint Venture "BrahMos", created for executing the works under the Project "BrahMos", and he has been one of the originators and was directly an active participant in creation of this organization and is irreplaceable mentor.

The development of missile complexes is related to realization of complete life cycle of a product from designing to trials and deliveries of production models of engineering.

All these stages of development are explicitly and interestingly described in the book. Significant attention has been given to flight trials of missile complexes from various platforms: land launchers, ship borne and underwater launch complexes by firing the missiles against different sea and land targets. These trials have validated high effectiveness and reliability of jointly developed missile technology. The missile became universal and capable to strike both sea as well as different land targets, and its combat capabilities are expanded.

In the book, much attention is given to Dr. A.P.J. Abdul Kalam and Gerbert Yefremov, who were holding the post of Director DRDO and

Director General NPO Mashinostroyenia respectively at the time of rolling out these activities, and the creation of Joint Russian-Indian organization for development of missile complexes was their idea and gave instrumental contribution in deployment and successful fulfillment of activities for realization of joint project.

It is necessary to mark that the writer has determined and stated the path and directions for further development of the project in this book, including development of infrastructures for expending production capacities, repair and maintenance, development of perspective missiles with improved characteristics.

I feel that the book proposed to the attention of readers will be extremely useful not only to the experts of Russia and India, who are working under military-technical cooperation, but also to the experts of other countries.

I would like to wish the author of the book and the team headed by him new successes and achievements in realization of joint project, which is important for our countries.

AG Leonov
Director-General
NPO Mashinostroyenia, Moscow

PREFACE

One day, after a phenomenally successful flight test of the BRAHMOS from a naval warship in the Arabian Sea, I was on a long journey sailing back towards the western coast of India near Goa. There was a celebration in the ship on the successful test. What a great system we have! It is flawless, precise, and the fastest. I returned to the captain's chamber, which was allotted to me for the journey, and started writing down notes on the missile's performance and the tasks lying ahead of us. All of a sudden, I thought I needed fresh air to dream further. So I went to the Bridge, on the top of the ship, and sat on the Fleet Commander's high raised chair covered with white cloth. I was alone on the Bridge and I started looking at the beauty of nature. The light cool sea breeze of the evening was embracing me. The setting sun's scattered rays glittered through the entire sea with their refracted light and as the sun started dipping, its orange rays went piercing the clouds. The dark blue but almost black sea hit the surface of the ship with its rhythmic waves and the water droplets fell on the deck. Shoal after shoal of gorgeous fish jumped out and went inside the water. It was now the transition to night. I looked up. The moon was rising and started spreading its shining milky-white light. Some stars started sparkling. I was in a different world. What a beautiful scene in the Arabian Sea!

Suddenly my mind stopped enjoying the beauty of the scene. All the past events that had led to the magnificent success of this missile project were running like a flashback in my mind. It all started with the bull's-eye hit on the decommissioned target ship by the missile, which travelled with multiple way points and made the target burn with its shear speed and leftover fuel. The results of the flight trial were like a textbook performance, achieving all the mission parameters and successfully eliminating the target. What a great feeling it was for the Indian Navy. The unified efforts of Indian and Russian scientists had resulted in the robust design of the missile, meeting the diverse requirements of the armed forces. The missile had stunned missile scientists across the world with its outstanding performance and reliability. Its high performance capabilities were par excellence when compared to any other cruise missile developed in the rest of the world. I was in an emotional mood. BRAHMOS had proved its superiority to the world—yet again.

So it was that after each successful launch the happiness of it engulfed me. The celebrations by the crew reverberated. Yet, this one time, the flight trial put me in a different mood. I started to recollect the initial days of the project and wonder what led to the success of the joint venture. Those initial days were the most productive days for the JV since the foundation of this mighty project was being laid and strengthened. The countless man-hours we spent gave a new dimension to the Joint Venture.

In 1995, when the idea to form a JV was crystallized, I was the programme director for the integrated guided missile development programme (IGMDP) and Dr Kalam suggested that I be the CEO and MD of the JV company, with the approval of the Government of India. Since I was a strong proponent for the entry of cruise missile in India and had worked for the formation of the JV from the beginning, I was the natural choice to lead the JV.

Many of my well wishers including senior bureaucrats were of the opinion that a JV with Russia could not lead to success and advised me not to take the responsibility. The main reason for their view was that the Soviet Union had broken up and the economic situation in Russia was declining rapidly during the 1990s. Moreover, the experiences of earlier JVs were not encouraging, especially in advanced technology areas because the risk was high in product realization. However, I was convinced that what I had learnt from the great visionaries – the 'men of honour' who laid the foundation for a technologically developed India and here I take the names of Dr Vikram Sarabhai, Prof. Satish Dhawan and Dr Abdul Kalam – would stand me in good stead. I was determined to face the challenges that might come my way.

Those visionary leaders had inculcated a wonderful culture that could bring about the desired results. Their way of encouraging even the small achievements of young engineers and scientists regardless of their positions and their soft way of pointing out mistakes are legendary. I was confident that by bringing together the great scientific minds of the two countries and with friendship and faith as the driving force, BrahMos could be an unprecedented success story.

I took charge as CEO and MD of the JV company BrahMos. This required me to carry out duties as both chief controller (R&D) for missile projects at DRDO and CEO & MD at BrahMos. And the duties of the two positions had to be carried out without any conflict of interest. Now, whenever I think back, I get goose bumps and cherish the memories of those hectic but fruitful days.

Today, the BrahMos joint venture between India and Russia is acclaimed all over the world as the most successful example of international defence cooperation. The sharing of expertise between the two countries in various missile technologies has made the missile the most powerful in its class. Scientists worked hand in hand right from the design phase to the production phase. The experiences that we all gained through the design, development, production and marketing stages are tremendous and mind-boggling. Today, many countries are requesting India to sell BRAHMOS missile system to them so that they can induct it in their armed forces. At the same time, many other countries including the powerful ones are worried. BRAHMOS supersonic cruise missile has been a great technological breakthrough, and it is all thanks to the innovative format of the joint venture.

Going back in time, we see that India had in the past excelled in the fields of mathematics, science, engineering, technology, medicine, astronomy and cosmology. There were many inventions too, though unfortunately there was no proper documentation, perhaps to discourage the replication and use of those achievements for evil purposes. Many engineering feats achieved in the early days are technologically at par with modern standards. Consider this dam at Tiruchirappalli District in the state of Tamil Nadu. It was built by Karikaal Chola, nearly 2,000 years ago. The dam, constructed as a barrage with just stones and mortar, resembles a snake's trail from an aerial view. Until the dam was reengineered by the British in the late 18th century, it was storing water for more than a millennium. Today the water flow has decreased due to the number of dams across the Cauveri and her tributaries in Karnataka and Tamil Nadu. But in those days, without these dams the water flow would have been enormous. How such a huge amount of water flow was diverted or how the dam was constructed is still not understood by experts. An extraordinary amount of human and animal effort would have been put in but we do not have any documentation of how such a feat in civil engineering was achieved. Similarly, the iron pillar at Qutub Minar standing for more than two millennia (912 BC) without rusting is a feat in metallurgy. There is, again, no document available to establish the composition of the pillar and how it was made.

Medical science was also at its zenith in ancient India. Acharya Sushruthis said to have conducted plastic surgeries in his time. Our *siddha*s were proficient in handling poisonous chemicals like mercury and arsenic to treat dreaded diseases such as cancer. They used the chemicals in a nano powder form (*pashpam*), which is proof that nanotechnology is not new to India. During the preparation of such medicines, managing the exhausts of poisonous fumes was necessary because inhaling them would result in death. To overcome such conditions, they used their Yoga skills and controlled their breathing.

Some of the chemical combinations, which they recorded in their scarcely available literatures, are found to be impossible to achieve even with modern advancements. There are records that they cured some terribly complicated diseases but we do not have any manuals on them. I have been witness to such medical miracle. As a 10-year-old boy, I had seen my father Mr Apathu Katha Pillai (meaning one who saves others from dangers), an expert in Siddha, Ayurveda and Yoga, curing dreadful diseases like cancer. Yet, like others of his ilk, he did not leave any record.

There were so many technological marvels, yet there are no documents regarding the process followed. Undoubtedly, India was dominating the world with its vast expanse of knowledge. But in the last one thousand years, the foreign invasions resulted in India plunging into her dark ages of slavery. Today, we have come a long way from the curse of slavery. We got freedom because of the sacrifice of the many, including the great leaders. But there is no war memorial at the capital to celebrate the freedom and how we got it and also to honour those great men. Today, our youth is full of enthusiasm to see a prosperous India. But they lack knowledge about the freedom movement and the greatness of our nation in the yester-years. Records should be maintained to help them to develop a sense of patriotism.

Coming back to the present, BRAHMOS is no small achievement. Everything started from scratch. Beginning with just the scope of an anti-ship missile development, we have created a universal missile. It is now a multi-platform, multi-target, multi-role and multi-trajectory-capable missile. In a record time of less than a decade, the missile has covered its journey from the drawing boards to deployment by the frontline forces. Certainly, BRAHMOS has made a page in the world history for its power and uniqueness.

So, there I was, at the celebrating naval warship in the Arabian Sea, sailing back towards the western coast of India, pondering upon the past. The captain informed me that the ship was about to reach the shore. After I reached the naval base, the thought that a book should be written on the BrahMos experience caught hold of my mind. If not written properly, our efforts and techniques will be forgotten in the future and the youth may have to reinvent what we already invented. And here I am today, with this book on BrahMos, whose equivalent is yet to be born.

The path that we travelled was not at all smooth. Many of our methodologies were daring and never attempted before. I hope that this book will be of much help for our future leaders, and that they will find in it inspiration to leap-frog their share of hurdles and constraints with courage.

Since the objective of the book is to reach everyone, I have not gone deep into technology intricacies. Of course, there is also the need to withhold critical aspects that relate to design and certain performances, this being a frontline weapon system for our armed forces.

I have used the metaphor of a voyage on the sea to narrate my experiences. Perhaps because the idea of the book first came to me – in a hazy sort of way – while I was travelling on a ship.

So, as we begin this voyage, let me just say this: records preserve knowledge, and it is knowledge that will help our progeny.

Dr A Sivathanu Pillai

ACKNOWLEDGEMENTS

The top leaders of the governments of India and the Russian Federation gave us outstanding support and constant encouragement, and played a significant part in the success of the joint venture. Visits by the presidents, prime ministers and defence ministers of both countries were a great source of motivation for Team BrahMos. BrahMos is always indebted to these leaders.

Our mentors and visionaries Dr APJ Abdul Kalam and Dr HA Yefremov through constant interaction, guidance and advice helped put the programme on the fast track. National Security Advisors, scientific advisors to the defence minister of India, directors of DRDO laboratories, secretaries to government, Indian industry captains, ambassadors of Indian and Russian embassies, and officials from Russia's Federal Service for Military-Technical Cooperation have been a constant source of encouragement. The chiefs of staff of the three wings of the Indian armed forces gave us outstanding support and pushed us to attain higher levels of performance, which led to continuous upgrade. Dr AG Leonov, Dr AA Dergachev, Mr AN Semaev, Dr AV Khromouchkin, Mr AN Strakhov, Mr AB Maksichev, Mr VM Kiselev, Mr VA Merkulov and many scientists from NPOM and partner Russian industries gave their all-out support to the programme.

Team BrahMos has a stellar cast of scientists, engineers, retired armed force officers and bureaucrats, supervisors, and technicians and staff from DRDO, NPOM and BrahMos. Their dedication and hard work have helped to shape the joint venture. They shared their experiences at every point of the growth trajectory of BrahMos, making the project a shining example of international cooperation.

While writing this book, many of my colleagues shared their experiences with me. A number of industry meets, partnership programmes and flight tests from ships and shores as well as interaction with administrators and service personnel became inputs for the book. I am thankful to all my colleagues and partners who contributed to this book, which is written on their behalf.

I specifically acknowledge the great innovative thoughts of Shri B Kamalanath, who has contributed towards the preparation of the book. His analysis of the Gulf War is remarkable. I am also thankful to Shri K Hariharan for his painstaking efforts and continuous improvisation of the text. Both these colleagues have worked many a day and night alongside me.

Finally, I thank my colleagues Shri Praveen Pathak, Shri Rohan Mishra and Shri Rupesh Verma, and of course Shri Rajan Arya of Pentagon Press for all their help.

Dr A Sivathanu Pillai

PART 1

Embarking on a Voyage

"To be secure on land, we must be supreme at sea."

– Pandit Jawaharlal Nehru
First Prime Minister of India

In this part, I will narrate two important incidents that turned the course for the Indian Navy – one a moment of jubilance and the other a mortal threat. The events led the Indian Navy to hunt for a superior weapon system. But that weapon system was nowhere to be seen. To possess such a weapon system, it was understood that an arduous voyage would need to be undertaken. The voyage was not just to be of the Indian Navy's but also of the nation...

1

A Battle on the High Seas

The Night of 4th of December 1971

Darkness had thrown its blanket on the buzzing Karachi harbour. Karachi, the headquarters of Pakistan Navy, had been an important naval base right from the colonial era. Movement of merchant vessel was restricted and a major portion of that area was under the grip of wartime darkness – Pakistan had started a war with India.

On the previous evening, Pakistan had mounted unsuccessful preemptive air strikes to neutralize the Indian Air Force (IAF) bases. Due to that, Pakistan was expecting an Indian retaliation from the air, virtually all over Pakistan.

At some time close to midnight, PNS *Khaibar*, a destroyer of Pakistan Navy patrolling that area, observed a bright light in the air approaching her. Since an aerial threat was expected, that bright light was assumed to be an attacking aircraft and the Pakistani sailors blazed away the vessel's anti-aircraft guns to shoot down the light. But that undeterred mysterious light kept coming closer and instead of dropping bombs, it rammed the vessel and exploded. Then, like a spike struck in the spine, the truth hit home –the light was not an aircraft but a missile. This was the first missile fired in anger in the Indian subcontinent. Before the Pakistanis recovered from their surprise and horror, a volley of missiles fired by three Indian warships attacked several Pakistani ships and set the harbour installations ablaze, celebrating a sort of Diwali (the Indian festival of lights). But these warships were just about bigger than fishing trawlers, and technically these were known as missile boats. The Indian Navy took pains in taking these small vessels near the enemy land and hitting them hard with Soviet SS-N-2B Styx missiles. The rest, of course, is history.

The Superpower Threat

The Indian Navy faced a grave threat from a superpower in the same war. The task assigned to the Indian Navy was to enforce a naval blockade to prevent vessel movements in both West and East Pakistan. The attack on Karachi was a part of this blockade enforcement. In the Bay of Bengal, the blockade was enforced through the task force centred on the aircraft carrier INS *Vikrant*. To intimidate India, a task force from the US Navy's Seventh Fleet was dispatched towards Bangladesh in support of Pakistan. It was headed by the nuclear-powered aircraft carrier USS *Enterprise*, the largest aircraft carrier in the world during that time.

The taskforce consisted of another small carrier carrying 25 assault helicopters and troops. These vessels were escorted by three warships armed with missiles, a nuclear attack submarine and four other vessels. The assignment was to break the blockade that had been imposed by INS *Vikrant* over the Bay of Bengal. The taskforce of INS *Vikrant* was no match for their American counterpart and was facing a formidable threat.

Yet, the much-hyped and awaited taskforce never swung into action. Later it came to be known that the Americans had turned away in the face of a powerful presence of Soviet nuclear submarines in the Indian Ocean, in support of India. The great threat was thus thwarted, thanks to the solidarity between India and the Soviet Union.

These two important incidents – a triumph and a threat – occurred in the 1971 Indo–Pakistan War. The Indian Navy began to think of a superior weapon system capable of engaging threats from a longer range. But this search was to go on for many years.

34 Years Later – 15th of April 2005

In the Arabian Sea, one of the Indian Navy's frontline warships INS *Rajput* was patrolling near Mumbai. The morning weather was pleasant and beautiful. Suddenly, at 0745 hours, the radar operator shouted, "enemy vessel!" The radar operator gave the bearing and range of the enemy vessel that was drifting towards Mumbai. The captain of INS *Rajput* was informed. He gave the necessary orders; bells started ringing and speakers screeched orders for the sailors to man their respective stations. Within minutes, the vessel was brought to a wartime state of alertness, with all the weapons ready to fire. Everybody's heart was thumping, because this could be a prelude to another war. The men of Indian Navy held their nerve due to their superior training. Anxious moments of waiting for the enemy to reverse their course were passing by. The enemy did not turn, they were advancing.

"Fire!" The captain ordered and in no time a missile took off from the deck of INS *Rajput*. The missile created a thunderous boom in the calm sea and it flew with a speed almost three times greater than the speed of sound. Like a thunderbolt, the missile struck the target vessel, which sank in minutes in two halves—as cinematographed in Hollywood movies. With this engagement, a new era dawned in the theatres of war.

The world's best supersonic cruise missile "BRAHMOS" had made its debut. Yes, the incident that I just described was a combat firing drill of the BRAHMOS missile and the vessel that was sunk was a decommissioned vessel of the Indian Navy, ex 'INS *Sindhudurg*. The entire drill was witnessed by the top echelons of the Indian Navy including Admiral Arun Prakash, the then chief of naval staff.

In combat, the enemy cannot even think of shooting down the BRAHMOS. What's more, they will not get to hear the thunder of the missile, because the missile is supersonic and stealthy. The sound is minimal while approaching the target. By the time the missile reaches the enemy, they will not be in a position to hear it, because they would have ceased to exist.

As expected, when the outcome of the combat firing drill was released to the media, it had our adversaries tying themselves up in knots. In the event of war, their warships may meet the same fate as that of the ex-INS *Sindhudurg*.

Today, the BRAHMOS supersonic cruise missile is progressively being inducted in the armed forces of India with constantly increased performance capabilities. The missile system was first inducted in the Indian Navy, then in the Indian Army, and finally in the Indian Air Force. The missile has become a frontline force-multiplier weapon system in the Indian armed forces.

Unlike in 1971, today the Indian Navy can fire missiles without moving closer to the enemy territory, yet inflicting a higher level of fatal damage. Plus, the Indian Navy does not need the support of an external power to counter superior threats. Even after over a decade of its first flight trial on 12 June 2001, there is no other equivalent weapon system on the horizon, either to match or to counter the BRAHMOS, even after over a decade of our first flight trial on 12 June 2001. That does not mean we can be complacent; technology always moves ahead. Hypersonic speed is the next level, and so on. It is necessary to think ahead and develop newer technologies that will maintain the edge in the war theatre.

PART 2

Unfurling the Sails

"...what all prudent princes ought to do, who have to regard not only present troubles, but also future ones, for which they must prepare with every energy, because, when foreseen, it is easy to remedy them; but if you wait until they approach, the medicine is no longer in time because the malady has become incurable."*

–Niccolo Machiavelli

*Prince = Country

The question is: why was India, a nation regarded as a peace pigeon by other countries, required to embark on the development of nuclear weapons and delivery systems (missiles)? In the next stage, how were these developed, and then how did they form the foundation for the BRAHMOS

2

Talons of a Pigeon – A Nuclear India

The reader must know why India speaks about disarmament and at the same time develops deadly nuclear missiles and possesses nuclear warheads. They must also know why nuclear India is a country with sufficient maturity and responsibility.

Concerns of India

What are the types of threats that a nation can face? Well, threats can be one or all of these in nature: economic, military, existential. Military threats severely undermine the military strength of a nation. Once the military is undermined, the nation is forced to be at the negotiation table, fighting unfavourable terms. As the strategist Karl von Clausewitz had said, "War is the continuation of policy (politics) by other means." It means that war is not merely an act of policy but truly a political instrument – a continuation of political activity by other (military) means. After WWI, Germany was made to cede territories and pay penalties through the Versailles Treaty dictated by the Allied Powers.

Generally, economic interests remain the driving force for conflicts and when favourable conditions are achieved by the conflict initiator, the conflict ends. Military threat can also originate from racial or religious hatred.

If the motivation is hatred, the enemy after destroying the nation's military may try to annihilate the population or occupy the nation itself. At this point the military threat transforms into an existential threat for a nation. For example, Israel faces existential threat from its surrounding nations. Since Israel is militarily strong and has the massive support of a superpower, it is able to blunt the threats and survive.

In that aspect, what are the threats that India faces?

For India, presently there are no threats, but there are concerns that can become threats. If we are sufficiently strong to handle any threat, then peace will continue to prevail and concerns will remain just that—concerns. But what are the concerns? There are two: one has its roots in the immediate neighbourhood and the other in the vicinity. The former is with regard to the military prowess and territorial claims of the neighbouring two countries that fought wars with India. In the vicinity we see proliferation of weapons and large-scale modernization of defence equipment. These proliferations can become a threat to India in future. As Niccolo Machiavelli says, "identification of threats at right time is important for future security." A comprehensive analysis of the threat perceptions and preparedness is essential for the defence of a country.

In the Neighbourhood

Chinese Territorial Claims

The root cause of troubles in the India–China relation is British India's and subsequently free India's perception of Tibet, vis-à-vis China's own perception of Tibet. During the British regime, the boundary between Tibet and India was marked and maintained through a border agreement. The agreement was based on the understanding that Tibet was an independent country and served as a buffer state. But the view of Communist China was that Tibet was a part of Chinese territory. China never accepted the demarcated border and maintained that Tibet was inside their territory.

China occupied Tibet by force in 1950. A huge transgression was made by China into Indian territory – Aksai Chin. Despite the uneasiness it caused, during the 1950s Chinese leaders assured India of a friendly relationship. This, though, did not stop the Chinese army from invading India and occupying many Indian positions in a brief border war during 1962. At present, not only does China still possess Aksai Chin, it also claims the Indian state of Arunachal Pradesh as theirs.

True, there is a massive amount of trade between India and China and the two countries have also adopted confidence-building measures. But the security concerns are a parallel reality too.

Militarily, China has almost three times greater might than India in terms of combat naval vessels, submarines, combat aircraft, artilleries, tanks and individual soldiers. China has a vast nuclear weapon stockpile and stands third after Russia and the USA. Not only nuclear weapons, China also has an array of nuclear-capable ballistic and cruise missiles. Further, the country has submarine-launched ballistic missile (SLBM) capabilities. Chinese missiles have multiple independent re-entry vehicle (MIRV) warheads, meaning that the missile's warhead will jettison many submunitions when it re-enters the atmosphere. Each submunition is also a nuclear warhead that can destroy a separate city. A single missile will be sufficient to pepper many enemy cities. Efforts are continuously on in China to perfect the ballistic missile technology to take it a step further.

Inimical Attitude of Pakistan

Immediately after Independence, the new nation Pakistan, keeping tribal proxies in the front, invaded Kashmir. Today a major portion of Kashmir is still under Pakistan as Pakistan-Occupied Kashmir. Further, Pakistan fought two full-blown wars during 1965 and 1971 and undertook what turned out to be a misadventure in the Himalayas in 1999, resulting in an armed conflict with India – known better as the Kargil War.

The military might of Pakistan can be levelled to a third of India's military might. This levelling, though, is for conventional forces only – that is, combat naval vessels, combat aircraft, artilleries, tanks, etc. On the unconventional front, Pakistan has nuclear-capable ballistic missiles. Pakistan is also aggressively developing nuclear-capable air-launched land-attack cruise missiles. Pakistan has an active nuclear programme and is reported to possess some 70–110 nuclear warheads. Arguably, Pakistan has developed these arsenals by compromising on economic development. Internationally it is feared that the deteriorating internal situation in Pakistan may lead to the terrorists getting control of nuclear weapons and missiles. In that case, the repercussions will be highly unpredictable and gravely serious.

On the other hand, the relationship between China and Pakistan is interesting. China had extended support to Pakistan during the 1965 and 1971 wars. The Pakistani nuclear programme benefited very much from Chinese assistance, both in nuclear weapons development and missile development. Many of the Chinese ballistic missiles reappear with a Pakistani name and colours.

In India, some feverish strategists claim that a two-front war scenario is on the rise. According to them, if Pakistan starts a war with India, then China may strike on the other border also. Similarly, if China starts a war with India, then Pakistan may also attack India. Further, the strategists believe that Pakistan's proxy war capability through its terrorist organizations may create additional troubles.

It should be noted that if these claims become true then India may have to fight from the marshes of Gujarat, the deserts of Rajasthan, the icy Himalayan heights and the less accessible north-eastern borders. Historically, two front wars have always been costly and deadly. It is worth remembering that during WWII when Germany was caught in a two-front war – with the USSR in the east and the other Allies in the west – its defeat became a certainty.

We do not know whether India may have to fight a two-front war with two nations armed with nuclear-tipped ballistic and cruise missiles. If such a situation occurs, it will be the worst threat that India can be tackling.

Concerns in the Vicinity: Proliferation of Weapons of Mass Destruction

The United States, the United Kingdom, Russia, France and China are the declared nuclear nations. They are the five permanent members of the UN Security Council and also referred to as P5. India attained nuclear capability in the year 1974 and became a self-declared nuclear weapon state in 1998. Pakistan also became a nuclear nation by 1998. There is the interesting case of Israel. Israel is suspected to have nuclear weapons but it has neither acknowledged nor denied this. So its nuclear status is not declared. North Korea and Iran are also in that status. Theoretically, Japan is just a step away from nuclear weapon development. Since Japan has all the technologies and expertise to build a nuclear weapon, it can build it quickly if required. Japan's Constitution, though, prevents it from building nuclear weapons.

When a nation possesses ballistic missiles – whether home-grown or proliferated or imported – it must be considered to be a 'concern' even if that nation is 'friendly'. Not only can that nation modify the missile, there is also the possibility of a sinister condition called the 'missile alliance'.

As long as missiles remain the frontline fighting teeth and the last line of defence, such missile alliances will keep on emerging. All such alliances have to be kept under a watchful eye. Reports say that Pakistan by transferring nuclear technology to North Korea received the Nodong missiles. Similarly, Iran's Shahab missiles have a distinct North Korean signature on them. Thus, every missile 'mass-produced' or 'bought' or 'proliferated' should be considered to be a 'threat'.

Weapons of mass destruction (WMD) are nuclear, biological and chemical (NBC) weapons that can bring significant harm to humans and can damage manmade structures. Ballistic missiles and to an extent cruise missiles are used as the delivery systems for these killers. These missiles take these warheads to the enemy territory to kill thousands in a go. A nation wishing to possess a dreadful WMD arsenal needs both delivery systems and the NBC weapons.

A conventional warhead is packed with high-explosive materials to cause destruction on a limited scale. The effectiveness of these warheads may be only for a few 100 metres. The NBC, or unconventional, warheads are meant for mass destructions – for killing civilians on an unimaginable scale.

Each of the three broad disciplines of science has one unconventional warhead: nuclear ones for physics, chemical ones for chemistry, and biological ones for biology. Biological warheads contain harmful micro-organisms like anthrax and can contaminate the target area, say a city, with these organisms. Such organisms multiply rapidly to cause highly contagious diseases, thus causing huge chaos and finally destruction. Imagine the chaos resultant of an entire city's population infected with these warheads and micro-organisms waiting to infect anyone who would enter the city. About 100 kg of anthrax spores can kill anywhere between 42,000 and 140,000 people. The USA possessed a huge arsenal of biological weapons and has since declared that it destroyed those stockpiles. India has no biological weapons and is a signatory to the Biological Weapons Convention that bans proliferation of biological weapons.

Chemical weapons release harmful chemicals. Chemicals like nerve agents can choke the nervous systems; some damage the respiratory systems; some blind the eyes; some can even lead to the decomposition of flesh. About 1,000 kg of the popular nerve agent sarin when dropped from air can kill anywhere from 400to 800 people. India possessed chemical weapons stockpilesbut has since destroyed them completely. India is also a signatory to the Chemical Weapons Convention that bans the proliferation of chemical weapons.

Clearly, a nation with a well-established biochemical technology base can develop both chemical and biological weapons. Expertise will be required in developing delivery systems and disperse mechanisms.

Theoretically, any nation that has an active nuclear programme for power generation can develop a nuclear weapon. How? Nuclear reactors using light waters as moderators need a specific uranium called enriched uranium, a highly radioactive isotope of natural uranium. This isotope exists in very, very small quantities in the natural uranium and has to be extracted. This process is called uranium enrichment. This very same enriched uranium can also be used for nuclear weapons. The key technology in nuclear weapons is getting this enriched uranium to become radioactive at a desired time and a desired place. To make the uranium radioactive, it must be compressed very hard. Usually it is done by explosive triggers. Thus, technology development and uranium-enrichment facilities can lead to nuclear weapon development.

WHAT DO WE INFER?

The P5 countries have a large number of nuclear weapons and carriers including intercontinental ballistic missiles (ICBMs). Such capability makes them powerful and gives them leverage to dominate world affairs. They are members of the UN Security Council. Countries like India, Pakistan, Iran, Israel and North Korea have nuclear weapons and intermediate-range ballistic missiles (IRBMs). There are 24 other countries that have short-range ballistic missiles of less than 1,000 km range. (The data is based on a study by Carnegie Endowment for International Peace.)

Today, India is surrounded by many countries that possess destructive weapons and have attained missile capabilities through imports and/or indigenous development. In particular, China and Pakistan who have fought wars with India possess nuclear weapons and long-range strike capability. The inference is that India cannot let itsguard down since the geopolitical tide may change at any time, translating proliferation activities into full-fledged threats.

DEALING WITH THE THREATS: INDIA'S ARMAMENT PROGRAMME

Going Nuclear

India attained independence from foreign occupation through the ahimsa principle. Never in the history of mankind had an entire nation stood up against the aggressors without weapons. India's weapon was new – it was satyagraha. In other nations, independence came at a terrible price.

Pandit Jawaharlal Nehru established a non-aggressive and tolerant foreign policy expressing brotherhood and peaceful co-existence. The policy framework was called Panchsheel–these five principles were to govern relationships between the new nations emerging after the colonial era. It was formally codified through a treaty between China and India in 1954. The five principles were:

1. Mutual respect for each other's territorial integrity and sovereignty
2. Mutual non-aggression

3. Mutual non-interference in each other's internal affairs
4. Equality and mutual benefit
5. Peaceful co-existence

In Nehru's words, "If these principles were recognized in the mutual relations of all countries, then indeed there would hardly be any conflict and certainly no war."

> During this period, India was in an enviable position in nuclear technology. This was achieved by the pioneering efforts of Dr Homi Jehangir Bhabha, who literally marshalled Indian nuclear energy efforts to the forefront. India's civilian nuclear energy efforts had the military aspect kept open. When Dr Bhabha died in an air crash in the year 1966, his responsibility was passed on to the hands of Dr Vikram Sarabhai. After the sudden demise of Dr Sarabhai in December 1971, Dr HN Sethna took charge of the development efforts and conducted the first nuclear test in 1974. Dr Raja Ramanna, who was instrumental in the nuclear test, became the chairman of Atomic Energy Commission and drew up a strategic map for the country.

Yet, in 1962 war was forced upon India. Following this war, China became nuclear in the year 1964. They also continued their programme ofmultiple missile development in a fast-track manner. By the mid-Sixties, their very first ballistic missiles, DF-1 and DF-2, became operational.

In 1965, Pakistan invaded Kashmir as part of what they called Operation Gibraltar. It led to a full-blown war that saw the defeat of Pakistan. By this time, Pakistan had started to get substantial Chinese material and diplomatic support. This relation seemed to have taken a leaf out of Chanakya's thesis that an adversary's adversary is a friend. Pakistan was also showing great interest in developing a nuclear weapon.

In the 1971 war between Pakistan and India, China again supported Pakistan. Before entering the erstwhile East Pakistan (present Bangladesh), Indian forces were required to substantially divert their resources to check the Chinese movements along the border. When Pakistan was comprehensively defeated and its territory dismembered, Pakistani-Chinese relationship had matured well enough to be described as a military alliance. Mr Bhutto, who became the leader of Pakistan in 1972, had proclaimed way back in 1965 that Pakistan had to go nuclear by all means. He was reported to have said, "Pakistanis will eat grass but make a nuclear bomb."

After the disastrous defeat of Pakistan, China is said to have aided Pakistan greatly and rendered support to subsequent actions required to go nuclear. The situation became critical. On one front was China, a nuclear and missile power. On the other front, Pakistan overtly wanted to become a nuclear-weapon state. The choice for India was clear.

The 'go' command for developing a nuclear weapon was given by the Indian Government. At the time when authorization was given, the technology for developing a nuclear bomb largely existed. Only the gaps needed to be plugged in. India conducted the first nuclear-weapon test in 1974. Further tests in 1998 made India a self-declared nuclear-weapon state. Both tests were possible because of the strong leadership and courage exhibited by the then prime ministers Mrs Indira Gandhi and Mr Atal Bihari Vajpayee, respectively. Yet the world must know India is the most responsible nation. India has never parted nuclear technology with any nation nor sold nuclear materials. The Indian nuclear policy is clearly defined.

India's Nuclear Doctrine

- **No first use:** In the event of war against a nuclear nation, India will not use a nuclear weapon first. But if attacked with a nuclear weapon, the enemy will receive a punishing strike beyond the level of imagination.
- **Non-usage on non-nuclear states:** India will never use a nuclear weapon on a non-nuclear state – unlike USA's nuclear attacks on Japan killing civilians in thousands in a flash.
- **Essential minimal deterrence:** The amount of nuclear stockpile maintained will be just sufficient to maintain a minimum deterrence.

Need for Delivery Systems

All over the world, during the Fifties and the Sixties, nuclear weapons were largely to be dropped only by aircraft. The Seventies saw the further development of air defence systems, which meant that in order to drop a nuclear bomb the aircraft had to penetrate the enemy air defence, go over the target and after surviving all of that, drop the bomb. Clearly, a viable and dependable means of nuclear-strike delivery was required, and that was ultimately the ballistic missile. In the Seventies, ballistic missiles had replaced long-range bombers and had been widely fielded by major powers.

India too needed ballistic missiles. But no nation would sell her such weapons after she had proved her nuclear capability. So it was that an indigenous, accelerated ballistic missile development programme was embarked upon.

3

In Pursuit of Missiles

India's continuous efforts to develop different types of missiles paid off. It was no small effort and the achievement was all the more laudable for it was without any technological assistance from other countries.

The Early Efforts

Defence Research and Development Organisation (DRDO) was formed in 1958 with Dr DS Kothari as the head. The objective of DRDO was to promote defence research in support of development of weapon systems and equipment for the Indian armed forces. Long before India opted for nuclear weapons, DRDO had embarked on missile projects since missile technology was a growing avenue.

In those early days itself, DRDO formed a Guided Missile Study Team that was later renamed as the Special Weapons Development Team (SWDT). The SWDT was to study the possibilities of guided missile development in India. Initially SWDT was located in New Delhi and later moved to Hyderabad in June 1962, as did Defence Research and Development Laboratory (DRDL). In later years, DRDL became the premier establishment for missile development.

SWDT came up with a feasibility study to develop a first-generation anti-tank missile (ATM) and the go-ahead was given. Preliminary work for developing the ATM began in the year 1964. The efforts picked up momentum in 1966, after the India–Pakistan War in 1965. During the next five years, a first-generation anti-tank missile was developed. The missile while flying would unspool a wire for its entire range of flight. An operator will direct the missile's flight through his console (something like a remote control). These steering commands will reach the missile's guidance system through the unspooled wire. The harder part was to track where the target was moving, apart from tracking where the missile itself was flying and then guiding it to hit the target. Although the missile went through several successful flights, the Indian Army was not interested since second-generation anti-tank missiles were available in the international arms market. That was the end of the indigenous ATM project.

A study was initiated on the design of a multi-stage surface-to-air missile (SAM). With support from Indian Air Force, in 1972 DRDL started a project called Devil. It was a surface-to-air missile based on the Soviet Union's SA-75 SAM system. The SA-75 was then being operated by the IAF. The development process of Devil was based on reverse engineering. A fresh missile would be disassembled and a particular section taken out. A replica of the section taken out would be developed by copying up to the degree of nuts and bolts. Then this replica would be integrated with the original missile. The missile would be fired and if it flew successfully the replica would be considered a success.

In due course of time, some contemporary components were used wherever possible. Slowly the entire missile components were developed. Finally, a stage was reached where an entirely new missile was developed by DRDL.

Despite the Devil flight trials achieving success, the project was closed in 1980. Together with the closure of the ATM project, this caused demoralization among the pool of missile scientists. On its part, the Public Accounts Committee (PAC) had begun their review of DRDL.

Dr Raja Ramanna from the Department of Atomic Energy (DAE) had taken charge as scientific advisor (SA) to the defence minister in 1978. He realized that the DRDL was not short of talent but it suffered for lack of leadership. He believed that with proper guidance DRDL would be able to complement the successes of Indian Space Research Organisation (ISRO) and Department of Atomic Energy DAE. ISRO had been regularly succeeding in its endeavours and the latest feather in its cap was launching of the Rohini satellite through the indigenously developed SLV-3. DAE had detonated the nuclear weapon successfully under Dr Ramanna's stewardship and was galloping ahead in many research areas in nuclear technology.

Dr Ramanna decided to put Dr Kalam, then project director of SLV-3, in charge of the missile development projects. That was a turning point.

I was working with Dr Kalam all through the successful days of SLV-3 at ISRO and his troubled period at Aerospace Design and Dynamics Group, Vikram Sarabhai Space Centre (VSSC). VSSC had formed a study group for a polar satellite launch vehicle (PSLV) and a configuration was evolved. The original proposed configuration by VSSC was a huge vehicle weighing 400 tonnes with two large strap-on boosters. Prof. Satish Dhawan realized that the proposed configuration was complex. He wanted to develop a reliable PSLV that would be the workhorse of ISRO and the core for future launch vehicle projects. He instructed Dr Kalam to come up with an alternate configuration for PSLV. After two years of continuous work under the guidance of Prof. Satish Dhawan, we evolved a configuration that was quite different and

In Dr Kalam's own words in his autobiography *Wings of Fire*:

"I recall my working at ISRO HQ, Bangalore, as director, launch vehicle programmes/ system, in the early 1980s, when we were debating the performance and cost-effectiveness of launch vehicles. In 1981, the scientists of VSSC, Thiruvananthapuram, with the help of other ISRO centres, evolved a configuration of the PSLV core vehicle with two large strap-on boosters. The PSLV weighed about 400 tonnes at take-off. Prof. Dhawan wanted to study an alternative and simple configuration. I and some of my colleagues, A Sivathanu Pillai, N Sundararajan and K Padmanabha Menon, carried out mission, technology and feasibility studies for the optimal configuration. The team designed several options, including a unique core vehicle with an advanced solid propellant booster, using first-stage rockets of SLV-3 as strap-ons. This brought the PSLV weight down to only about 275 tonnes at take-off."

much lighter. Today, I am happy that this configuration has become the mainstay for ISRO to make successful launches injecting satellites in the polar orbits.

We were also thinking of a missile project called 're-entry experiment' (REX). Dr Kalam wanted to convert the SLV-3 into a missile but Prof. Dhawan wanted to keep ISRO away from missile development as it might affect the international cooperation that ISRO had from many countries. Yet, Dr Kalam's mind was fixated on developing a re-entry class of missiles. Indeed he did that, not in ISRO but in DRDO. Do you know what missile was that? It was none other than the Agni.

Dr Kalam reminisces in his *Wings of Fire*:

> "Meanwhile, I carried out an analysis of the application of SLV-3 and its variants with Sivathanu Pillai, and compared the existing launch vehicles of the world for missile applications. We established that the SLV-3 solid rocket systems would meet the national requirements of payload delivery vehicles for short and intermediate ranges (4,000 km). We contended that the development of one additional solid booster of 1.8 m diameter with 36 tonnes of propellant along with SLV-3 subsystems would meet the ICBM requirement (above 5,500 km for a 1,000 kg payload). This proposal was, however, never considered. It nevertheless paved the way for the formulation of the Re-Entry Experiment (REX) which, much later, became Agni."

At ISRO, in spite of the SLV-3's success, Dr Kalam was facing frictions. He was thinking of moving to missile development – something that Prof. Dhawan did not approve of. Dr Kalam wrote a handwritten letter to Prof. Dhawan expressing, "My heart is on missiles and I want to go." Dr Raja Ramanna took his successor Dr VS Arunachalam in confidence about Dr Kalam. Dr Arunachalam approached the then defence minister Mr R Venkataraman and Dr Kalam was thereafter appointed to DRDL. A new era in Indian missile development began.

THE IGMDP

At DRDL, Dr Kalam chaired the Missile Study Team (MST) to develop the types of missiles required for the Army, the Navy and the Air Force. The team, which included members from R&D, production and services, zeroed in on five projects – SS-150, SAM-X, tactical core vehicle, third-generation anti-tank missile and re-entry technology demonstrator– to be undertaken as part of the Guided Missile Development Programme (GMDP). They prepared a feasibility study and presented it to Dr VS Arunachalam, the then chiefs of armed forces and Defence Minister Mr R Venkataraman. The defence minister instructed that the missiles be developed concurrently instead of sequentially. Hence, the project name was modified to Integrated Guided Missile Development Programme (IGMDP).

The Five Projects of the IGMDP

- SS-150: A tactical surface-to-surface missile (150 km range) for the Army; later named Prithvi
- Multiroletactical core: A multirole missile system for the Army, the Navy and the Air Force; later named Trishul
- SAM-X: A surface-to-air missile (25 km) with multi-target handling capability for the Army and the Air Force; later named Akash
- ATM-3: An advanced third-generation anti-tank missile for the Army; later named Nag
- RTV: A re-entry test vehicle to develop re-entry technology; later named Agni (the technology demonstrator was later developed into a full-fledged weapon system)

The programme was formally sanctioned by the Government in July 1983 with a time frame of 12 years.

The task of developing five missiles simultaneously and within a short span of time was not easy. It required a great deal of reorganization within DRDL. During this critical period Dr Kalam visited Bangalore frequently. He did this to meet his ISRO friends in Bangalore and especially to meet me to discuss the various techno-managerial issues of IGMDP, more often than not over lunch at the Woodland Hotel. In due course he made me a part of his decision-making process and wished that I could join him in the missile group.

Prof. Dhawan, who had been grooming me, rejected the suggestion from Dr Kalam on many occasions and always informed me that he did so. For Dr Kalam on the other hand, having worked at ISRO with its flexible environment, it was extremely difficult for him to adapt to a regimented DRDL. Many a times he expressed his worries. He needed the help of ISRO in terms of technology reviews by experts, using the solid booster of SLV-3 for Agni, using the Sriharikota range for launching missiles, and so on. Fortunately, my availability at ISRO HQ enabled him to get all the required support.

After Prof. Dhawan, Prof. UR Rao became the chairman of ISRO. This time around, both Dr Kalam and Dr Arunachalam were successful in getting me to DRDL on deputation. When I arrived at DRDL, the design process was just over for the Prithvi and Agni missiles. As yet, though, a lot of development tasks were required to be done to accelerate the projects.

I became the director of planning and programme analysis. The purpose was to give a new accelerated thrust to technology development, networking among groups as well as programme management for the five projects. I was required to help Dr Kalam to restructure DRDL into a unique matrix set-up. In this new structure, project directors were empowered with more administrative and financial powers, as it was in ISRO. In DRDL the programme management culture did not exist. My ISRO experience and working closely with Dr. Kalam came in handy to bring an effective programme management system that could help to streamline critical technology development process. In a multi-project environment with limited resources and conflicting interests, programme management was very much essential to achieve the objectives of the IGMDP.

What were the objectives of the IGMDP?

As delineated by Dr Kalam, once the missile was developed, it should demonstrate contemporary performance at the time of deployment and have these features: a) futuristic in terms of concept and technology, b) possessing different capabilities (multirole), and c) of practical value to the Army, the Navy and the Air Force (multi-user).

Futuristic

The sad history of the Devil and ATM projects was not to be repeated. In their case the technology was already obsolescent when the development started. When the development ended and a weapon system matured, they had ultimately become obsolete. Moreover, the systems available with the armed forces were already obsolescent because no nation provided to another nation a weapon system of the same class and quality used by its own armed forces. Only export-quality systems with inferior performance were offered to other countries.

> **What is export quality in arms market?**
>
> In commercial commodities, export quality is the most superior quality possible for that commodity. But in the arms market, export quality means a degraded version of the original weapon system. Secondly, a huge amount is charged for those systems that command a high demand in the world market.

By working on a futuristic system, the Indian armed forces would get a superior and contemporary system at the time of deployment of that weapon system. It meant that there was a need to leapfrog technologies, deviating from the beaten path, for which new concepts, design methodologies and management approaches had to come together.

Multirole and Multi-user

A single system can be used for various missions. This benefits both the producer and the user. For the producer, he gets more jobs and hence more profit. For the user, he gets the advantage of cost reduction due to the mass production. The user can maintain a large force level and need not use different systems for different missions. The training and maintenance aspects become simpler. Instead of maintaining different types of systems in his inventory, he can just maintain a single type.

We decided that all the five missiles must have multirole capability. For example, the Trishul missile had three roles: of being an anti-aircraft missile (ground to air), an anti-seaskimmer (missile fired from ship against anti-ship missiles), and an anti-radar missile (air to ground). In fact, this is how it got its name, meaning the three-bladed 'trident'.

Similarly, Prithvi – so named because it is a surface-to-surface missile – has field-interchangeable warheads, where the users can choose warheads and fix these in the field according to the type of targets to be neutralized. Prithvi can be used from a mobile launch system on ground or from a ship against land targets, and is relevant for all the three services. The medium-range surface-to-air missile Akash is on tracked vehicles and wheeled vehicles and suitable for use by the Army and the Air Force, respectively. It was so named as the theatre of war is in the sky (*akash*). Nag is a third-generation anti-tank missile that can be launched from a tank or from a helicopter. The long-range Agni has to go into space and re-enter the atmosphere. At the re-entry point, the missile module experiences a very high temperature of more than 2500°C – which is equivalent to Agni Pravesh and hence the name Agni.

Constraints and Difficulties

In the 1980s when we were starting the IGMDP, the technological gap was enormous. The technology-time gap was more than 30 years as compared to the developed nations. During the Cold War between the Soviet Union and the USA, the technological progress was tremendous.

The colonial rule had kept India away from the Industrial Revolution. This had serious implications in terms of non-availability of suitable industries in India for taking up major missile development programmes. The post-1962 Indo–China war was the licensed production era. Only the necessary knowledge to manufacture would be passed on by the producer nation to defence public sector units. This meant that the industry would have only 'know-how' capability, not the 'know-why' capability. The only encouraging factor for India was the thrust given by Prof. Satish Dhawan for industries to participate in the space programme. ISRO's contribution to create a minimal base for aerospace technology products would prove valuable for the IGMDP.

Missile Technology Control Regime (MTCR)

Simply put, it is the 'technology denial regime' enforced by First World nations. MTCR is an informal and voluntary association of various countries to prevent the proliferation of unmanned delivery systems capable of carrying a 500 kg payload (read nuclear warheads) to 300 km. MTCR seeks to coordinate restrictions in exports of complete rocket systems, unmanned air vehicles and related technology.

Unfortunately, some of the systems and technologies having greater civilian applications are also denied or come with a strong end-user agreement that it would not be used for any military purpose. The MTCR was originally established on 16 April 1987 by Canada, France,

Germany, Italy, Japan, the UK and the USA. The Russian Federation became a signatory in 1995.

The MTCR has a long list of technologies and systems that are banned for exporting. Some common systems like the computerized tomographic scanning systems (commonly known as CT scans) come with an end-user certificate. If the system is found to be used for military purpose, that organization will be blacklisted and denied further imports. Many of the military-grade computing processors are also restricted by this regime. However, all such transfers are considered on a case-by-case basis (read: nations that are supported by the big powers can import these technologies and proliferate their missiles).

India is not a signatory to the MTCR and many other controversial treaties like Non-Proliferation Treaty (NPT) and Comprehensive Test Ban Treaty (CTBT). Hence, many technologies that could have been easily procured from abroad were denied to us. When some technology or equipment is available, it makes sense to use it straightaway. On the other hand, developing the same is time-consuming and calls for 're-inventing the wheel'.

In hindsight, what must have seemed to be a curse at one point turned out to be the proverbial 'blessings in disguise'. India developed all the technologies that were denied to her, turning the situation into a classic case of 'technology denied is technology gained'.

But how did that happen?

To begin with, nearly 200 technology packages were identified to be developed for the success of the IGMDP. All these packages were developed for the first time in India. Failure in developing these would directly result in the failure of the IGMDP itself. Building critical technologies was full of challenges, because they were new and the base knowledge was insufficient. Knowledge, manpower, infrastructure and industrial support had to be made available in the required manner, according to the technology being developed and its relevant importance in the IGMDP. The progress of the development had to be constantly reviewed and problems had to be solved in real time.

Technology empowerment became possible through a consortium approach and also through collaborative partnerships among the identified partners from R&D labs, academic institutions and industries. Those activities had to be planned and strategically managed in order to realize the critical technologies. Above all these measures, we had to be innovative. When we went off the beaten tracks, success came like a fruit dropping on to our laps.

Leap-Frogging through Innovations

Let me take the reader through two important technology developments in India combating the MTCR – namely re-entry heat shield for Agni and guidance system for Prithvi. These developments ultimately raised our technological capabilities to international standards, paving the way for joint ventures.

Re-Entry Heat Shield for Agni

When a ballistic missile reaches the edge of the atmosphere (assume an altitude of 100 km), the warhead gets separated and starts descending towards the target. While falling, it re-enters the atmosphere at a speed greater than 10 mach (1 mach = 330 m/s). The warhead experiences stiff air resistance and due to the resulting friction it gets heated up to a mammoth 2,500°C. When we speed up even in ordinary buses and motorbikes we can feel the air resistance in headwinds. Imagine the friction at a speed greater than 10 times the speed of sound.

The warhead contains explosives that may be conventional or nuclear material. If such heat is allowed to seep inside, the warhead would go useless. So, thermal insulators are required to protect the warhead from heating. I hope one will never forget what happened to Kalpana Chawla. She and her crew were returning to the earth in the space shuttle *Columbia*. At the time of re-entry, the failure of thermal insulators resulted in the loss of the shuttle and the crew.

Now, how to develop such thermal insulators? Since metals generally melt and evaporate at these high temperatures, such insulations are possible through carbon-based composite materials for the structure and carbon-carbon composite material for the tip. This material has the ability to ablate at high temperatures and high velocity in a uniform manner. Due to this the flight trajectory is maintained, protecting the warhead by maintaining the temperature at less than 50 °C. This technology is essential for long-range missions like intercontinental ballistic missiles (ICBMs) or manned space missions. Re-entry technology is therefore a highly guarded secret for the few nations possessing it. In India, a team of scientists headed by Mrs Rohini Devi took it up as a challenge and successfully developed the re-entry technology.

While developing any flying machine, how can we know about the aerodynamic behaviour of it? One option is to test the scaled-down model in wind tunnels. In the tunnel the model is kept stationary and air is blown on it at the speed with which that vehicle is expected to fly. The flying conditions are simulated at various speeds at which the vehicle is expected to fly. Various aerodynamic performance parameters like the drag at particular spots in the body are studied to validate the design.

Now recall the trajectory of a ballistic missile; the vehicle re-enters the earth's atmosphere at hypersonic speed. To validate the aerodynamics of the nose tip, we needed a hypersonic wind tunnel – one that would blow air at hypersonic speed. We did not have such a facility.

The other option was to arrive at the optimum shape through computational fluid dynamics (CFD), which would help to validate the aerodynamic design of a flying machine. The aerodynamic design comprises of thousands of grid points; assume these grid points as nodes in the skeletal structure. CFD software validates the design by calculating the mathematical parameters of each grid point. But before the advent of computers, they were all done through mathematical calculations. Manual mathematical calculations for nose-tip evaluation would require years to complete. In the 1980s we had just stepped into the information age and mathematical calculations were done in desktop PCs, which required at least nine days for evaluating and optimizing one grid point in the nose tip among thousands of grid points. We required a supercomputer. That, though, was easier said than done. The US-made supercomputer Cray X-MP was available at Indian Meteorological Department but was used for weather prediction.

Now came the hindrance; the computer was procured from the US but with the restriction that it should not be used for any other (read as defence) purpose. So, in spite of the availability of the machine, we were unable to use it. Dr VS Arunachalam, the then chief of the organization, and Dr Kalam, the then chief of missile programme, went to the US and made a request to Defence Secretary Mr William Parry for permitting the use of the existing supercomputer or agreeing to sell a new one for defence R&D purposes. Mr Parry gave a good lunch to them but not the supercomputer. Returning with empty hands, Dr Arunachalam established the Advanced Numerical Research and Analysis Group (ANURAG) with Prof. G Venkataraman deputed from Indira Gandhi Centre for Atomic Research (IGCAR), Kalpakkam, as the leader to design and develop a supercomputer for undertaking the Agni re-entry module design. The time given was 24 months.

Imagine the scenario some 25 years ago. That was a time when ordinary calculators were treated like computers by the general public of India. When there was no indigenous capability to develop an ordinary computer, could we hope to develop a supercomputer?

Well, Dr Venkataraman, Dr Neelakantan and 14 youngsters developed a hypercube-based parallel processing supercomputer for the CFD analysis. In the meantime, another group was established at Indian Institute of Science (IISc) headed by Prof. Deshpande to develop new software codes for the CFD.

Finally, in the assigned 24 months, a 32-node parallel computer called PACE+ was developed with a capacity of 1.7 gigaflops. Roughly, one flop can be compared to one calculation. PACE+ was capable of executing 1,700,000,000 floating-point operations per second. It was 20 times faster than the Cray X-MP that was refused to us. With the combination of PACE+ and the new software codes for CFD, each iteration got reduced to just five minutes from the earlier nine days.

The nose-tip model was evaluated and cleared for integration with the missile. The irony was that after the development of our supercomputer, the US offered us their Cray X-MP. The offer was promptly declined. Today we have mastered the re-entry technology and Agni has got various versions with ranges from 700 km to 5,000 km. Thus, innovatively developing the supercomputer and the usage of home-grown software paved the way for success.

Inertial Guidance System for Prithvi

Prithvi is a uniquely designed short-range ballistic missile. It is not that we were the first to develop a short-range ballistic missile. Many countries had achieved that much ahead of us. So then, what makes the Prithvi unique?

What is manoeuvrable trajectory?

Earlier, ballistic missiles were designed to fly in the conventional parabolic trajectory. When a ballistic missile is inbound for an attack, the enemy missile defence system tracks it continuously and predicts its trajectory. Then it calculates a suitable interception point. It launches its anti-ballistic missile (interceptor missile) such that at this point the interceptor missile either collides or blasts near the incoming missile to destroy it. For all these activities, the enemy has a very, very short time window, failing on which the incoming missile will finish its job. For the interception to be perfect, the missile defence system's accurate tracking is very important.

For the IGMDP objective, the 'futuristic' Prithvi should be able to evade anti-ballistic missiles. For that, Prithvi has to manoeuvre. A cruise missile can manoeuvre, but for a ballistic missile the manoeuvring will be very difficult.

So, the scientists give wings to Prithvi. With the wings, Prithvi gains both yaw and pitch manoeuvring. Because of this manoeuvre, the enemy missile defence system will not be able to either predict the trajectory of the incoming Prithvi missile or determine Prithvi's targets.

It is the manoeuvrable trajectory. Prithvi has to manoeuvre and also be highly accurate to reach the target, which is decided by the accuracy of the guidance system. Such guidance systems are entirely dependent on the high-precision navigational sensors. Again, this was not available to India. Without the sensors there was no possibility for developing a high-accuracy guidance system. Four young scientists were given the task to come up with a solution that would help attain better accuracy using the rudimentary gyroscopes that were being produced at Hindustan Aeronautics Limited (HAL).

This led to the great idea of error compensation. The group of young scientists studied the sensors, did several mission runs to characterize the sensors, and calculated the errors at various stages of flight. The simulation of the trajectories including many perturbations and failure modes was carried out to estimate the error bands. The idea was to compensate the error by making the guidance computer understand the error. When the computer understands the error, it compensates for the error. How to compensate was instructed through the software so as to give better accuracy at the end of the flight.

The system had got validated in hardware-in-loop simulation and later in the flight trials. The innovation of compensating the hardware-induced error through software played a key role in realizing an excellent inertial guidance system.

The End Result of IGMDP

The IGMDP made India self-reliant in strategic missiles-Prithvi and Agni in various versions. She now had the competence to design and develop any type of tactical missiles, and most importantly the availability of critical technologies, missile scientists and relevant infrastructure. Akash had gone through several successful flight trials and accepted by the Indian Air Force for induction. Many off-shoot missiles came out of the IGMDP.

Programme Management: The Key to Success

IGMDP started as a multi-project missile development programme but due to the unavailability of the required technologies, it became a vast technology development programme intertwined with missile development. This intertwining made it one of the most complicated technology development programmes in the world. The technologies were new and futuristic. However, the technology base at DRDL itself was very limited. So a large number of government labs, academic institutions and private and government industries had to be brought together. The technologies were to be developed at multiple institutions and laboratories with networked organizations. While today we have the Internet that brings all the information to the table, back then computers were primitive with monochromatic monitors displaying green fonts in a black background and these could be operated only in air-conditioned rooms. We had to find various industries, research laboratories and academic institutions manually, through reports or personal contacts.

Uncertainties, complexities, different working cultures and attitudes, difficult procedures, the military environment and the attendant secrecy–all attacked IGMDP at the same time. Keeping these constraints in mind, the DRDL management was reorganized as a matrix structure. In a nutshell, in the evolved structure a systems manager oversaw the technology development in his regime, while a project director took care of the entire missile project. They reported to the programme management board that oversaw all the five missile projects.

Effective control was established through the matrix structure. It helped to resolve conflicts, assign priorities, avoid duplications and stick to the schedule.

Inherent complexities of technology development, gave a real challenge for effective management. The complexities were multi-faceted – Networking of establishments and related management, Time criticality and Technology criticality and so on. Above all the multiple technology developments were intertwined with multiple missile developments.

Networking of establishments and activities monitoring was a hectic process in IGMDP. Today, we have internet that brings the world in our finger tips. But in those days internet was just a concept in India. In those days, computers were primitive with monochromatic monitors displaying green fonts in a black background and being operated only in air conditioned rooms. Even a television was a rarity, a home with an antenna (dipole antenna) served as navigation references in residential areas. The younger generation would not have heard about these antennae lest to see. Today it is the era of DTH with DVD quality video and audio. In that era, we had to find various industries, research laboratories and academic institutions manually through reports or personal contacts. We had to understand their expertise and capabilities and to delegate works and take them along with us.

In the IGMDP, we were developing more than 200 critical technologies and many sub-critical technologies, in addition to other less critical but important technologies. Everything was time-bound and we had to manage about 22,000 activities including technology research, technology development and product manufacturing. All these activities were carried out across the length and breadth of India.

Remember the communication facilities existed in India. People who have born after 90s may not be aware of the India of 80s. Owning a telephone or a television was a luxury and those who were financially affluent were able to afford them. Cars - they were a rarity unlike today where a person can buy a car and park it in his garage within a day. But those days one had to wait indefinitely for buying a car.

The programme management directorate at DRDL monitored 22,000 activities comprising of research, development, production and testing that were being executed at various places across India. We had to receive reports on all those activities at the month-end, analyze them, understand the progress and difficulties, and address them. While giving corrective measures on the deviations or issues, we had to also issue the next tasks in those activities for the forthcoming month.

All those activities were time-critical. All the development activities for a particular missile must coincide at a predetermined time.

The missile development was time bound; almost each subsystem required some sort of technology development for it. The development of the missile cannot be stopped for want of that particular technology dependent subsystem. Worst case was, there could be so many subsystems requiring so many technologies for a missile.

Each second wasted would reduce considerable percentage of the user's confidence on DRDO's capability to deliver the missile – Just not one missile but five missiles. Along with the development of required technologies, it is essential to manage and solve personal issues, morale issues, material requirements, bureaucratic hassles, etc. It required an overall control scheme of the programme. The evolution of that scheme itself is a great outcome of IGMDP.

I will highlight some of the techniques used to progress IGMDP, using a great lot of experience I gained in launch vehicle projects at ISRO. We introduced different strategies for critical technology development, monitoring of large activities through a computer aided scheme, critical activity monitoring scheme with clear cut milestones. Conflict resolution in multi project environment with PACE technique, structured review system, flight trial mission management, capability build up, infusing technology skill, capacity build up by large scale induction of scientists reducing the average age of the organisation, continuous renewal by re-organisations in 1986, 1989, and 1992. The above activities introduced a new culture and a movement to achieve results. The seeds laid 25 years before in DRDL, have resulted in many young scientists managing huge missile projects and as Directors of laboratories today, and many generations will follow.

An Unfinished Job

For the IGMDP, we concentrated on strategic offensive missile systems and tactical defensive missiles. Though initially conceived as a tactical missile, due to various reasons Prithvi became a strategic missile. In a war, a strategic missile will be the final weapon of choice. In the initial stages, a strategic missile will not be used as it may give a wrong message. The enemy may not know what the strategic missile is carrying. It may be carrying a non-nuclear warhead but the enemy will very likely assume that the incoming missile is carrying a nuclear warhead. So he will retort with his nuclear missile strike.

A strategic missile serves only one purpose: deterrence. It is a message for the enemy that if he fires his strategic missile then we will also fire ours to finish him off. With ICBMs in their arsenal, the USSR and the USA never fired them during their Cold War games. Now imagine this: if Prithvi is fired in a war with a non-nuclear warhead, the enemy will still regard the missile as a nuclear attack. Eventually he will retaliate and he will also have the excuse that he was only retaliating. Not only that, we will be held responsible for provoking him though we had only launched a non-nuclear missile on him.

The other missiles of IGMDP were purely defensive with the exception of Nag, which however could engage only tanks. Overall, a wide gap was observed – that an indigenous tactical war-winning missile was absent in our country. A missile system that could be the 'first-strike weapon system' was needed. Our missile team often used to discuss this issue and tried to find a solution. Yet, we were not able to determine what that first-strike weapon would be.

PART 3

In Uncharted Waters

"Continuous effort – not strength or intelligence – is the key to unlocking our potential."

– Winston Churchill

There was no trail for us to follow. BrahMos was the first JV for a military system in India. The JV was also the first of its kind to design, develop, produce and market a futuristic supersonic missile through an intergovernmental agreement. To achieve our goals, we had to find our own path.

4

LEAPFROGGING

THE FASTEST MISSILE

When I returned to India from Harvard Business School in May 1991, the Persian Gulf War had almost ended. I made a detailed study of how the Tomahawk missiles played an impressive role in the war. Our missile team was eager to develop a cruise missile and ballistic missile defence system. We were in favour of using the Akash as a BMD weapon for terminal-stage engagement and developing a cruise missile, both with the support of other countries. The collaborative model paved the way for several teams to visit us and in turn allowed us to analyze the BMD capabilities of other countries, especially Russia, France and Israel. IGMDP had delivered outstanding results at that time with many critical technology building blocks, in spite of the missile technology control regime and technology denials. The technological strength of India was no longer in doubt.

For the cruise missile, the team started looking at various options in terms of propulsion, guidance and control, seeker and configurations. The members took up this task as an extra effort apart from their regular tasks. As per the benchmarks set for IGMDP, we wanted this new missile to be futuristic and the best in its class at the time of deployment. The point as usual was 'how'. An answer came during one of our brainstorming sessions – it was to simply 'increase the speed'. In what way increased speed will make the missile futuristic? When the speed of attack increases, it automatically reduces the response time of the enemy. At that time, all the operational cruise missiles in the lead countries were flying only at subsonic speeds.

The Gulf War: How the Tomahawks Got the KARI

The war was fought from 2 August 1990 to 28 February 1991, between Iraq and a UN-formed coalition force of 34 nations. The conduct of the Persian Gulf War is a lesson in electronic warfare and air power. It was a war between a formidable air defence system and a formidable air force. Above all, it was a war where precision-strike cruise missiles won the day for the coalition force. This war was like a primer for the conduct of future wars.

The Iraqi forces were very strong, comprising of approximately 1.2 million ground troops, more than 5,000 tanks and 3,500 artillery weapons. After occupying Kuwait they had fortified their defences along the Saudi–Kuwait border and the Iraqi seashores.

To evict the Iraqi forces from Kuwait, the coalition ground forces had to face the Iraqi ground forces head-on. But engaging Iraqi ground forces would have resulted in huge casualties for coalition ground forces. That level of casualties would be unacceptable to the western countries on political grounds. Moreover, Saddam declared that Iraq would attack Israel if Iraq was attacked. This would have forced Israel to retaliate against Iraq. Saddam's calculation was that such a situation would make other Arabian nations withdraw from the coalition due to their bitter enmity with Israel. Withdrawal of the Arab nations from the coalition would have resulted in coalition forces being denied territories to launch military offensives against Iraq.

Overall, for the coalition forces the war had to be won quickly before Iraq, with its known chemical warfare capability, could do any damage to Israel. Not only that, the war had to be won without escalating the war itself.

The coalition decided to employ airpower to blunt the strength of the Iraqi forces. One of their strategic moves was to disrupt the 40 or more command and control (C2) centres situated throughout Iraq. A robust communication network is as essential as the command centre itself. This communication network functions through communication nodes like microwave relay towers and telephone exchanges. Destruction of these nodes would destroy the network and it would be impossible for the higher commands either to receive situation reports or to pass orders. The lack of clear orders will make the frontline defence crumble due to lack of clear orders.

The other target groups for the coalition forces included electricity production and oil refining facilities, naval forces and port facilities and airbases; NBC weapons research, production and storage facilities; Scud missile production, storage and launch preparation facilities; and railroads and bridges that were the supply lines for Iraqi troops in Kuwait. Many of the telephone lines and fibre optic cables were also laid along these bridges and destruction of these bridges would serve two purposes: denial of transportation and denial of communication link.

Saddam knew that the coalition forces would resort to air power. And he was ready to face that with a robust air defence system. The coalition found that it was not easy to destroy the predetermined targets due to the presence of a gigantic Iraqi integrated air defence system (IADS), also known as KARI. The KARI served as an aerial fortress to protect this air space. This system had virtually turned the Kuwaiti and Iraqi airspace into killing fields for coalition aircraft. The KARI consisted of air defence systems (ADS) like anti-aircraft artillery (AAA) and surface-to-air missiles (SAM). These air defence systems complemented each other and provided mutually overlapping coverage. Thus, an aircraft trying to destroy one ADS could be engaged by the neighbouring ADS.

The IADS was so constructed that any neighbouring ADS belonged to a different genre or was of a different operational frequency/ modulation or was of a different national origin. This arrangement served to degrade electronic warfare capabilities of the coalition forces. (Jamming is an important feature of electronic warfare. So, if the attacking aircraft tries to jam an ADS, the adjacent ADS will be unaffected by this jamming because of its entirely different nature. The adjacent ADS will be able to engage the attacking aircraft efficiently.) Above all, each and every ADS was connected to a command centre called Intercept Operations Centre (IOC). There were many such centres, which in turn were connected with a Sector Operations Centre (SOC) that looked after the air defence operations of some two or three IOCs. All of these SOCs were connected to a central Air Defence Operations Centre (ADOC) situated at Baghdad under the direct control of Saddam. The ADOC was duplicated by some 40 centres situated in Baghdad itself. The arrangement was such that even if one of the centres was destroyed, another centre could take over the operations without any degradation. The greatest advantage was that without using its individual radar system an ADS could engage attacking aircraft (once it turned on its radar, its location would be revealed to the attacking aircraft, which could then destroy it).

Not surprisingly, the KARI itself became a primary target for the coalition forces. The complication was that the KARI was there to destroy the very same aircraft meant to attack it. An alternate potent weapon other than aircraft was required. That weapon was the Tomahawk cruise missile.

The coalition forces struck their first blow at about 03:00 hours local time on 17 January 1991. The coalition aircraft took off to attack. But before this wave of attack, the Tomahawk cruise missiles were launched from US Navy's surface vessels and submarines. These missiles bypassed the air defence sites to hit the C3 nodes at very low altitudes. As many as 50 Tomahawk cruise missiles were fired against key military command-and-control posts and government buildings.

In the first few hours itself the KARI was almost degraded. And in the first few days, KARI almost ceased to exist. After this phase, the coalition aircraft targeted the frontline troops in Kuwait, tanks, artillery, supply vehicles, bridges, etc. Most importantly, they destroyed the morale of Iraqi soldiers, who were deprived of their own aerial support, food, medicine and ammunition. After 40 days of continuous bombardment from air, the coalition ground forces swung into action. They started from Saudi Arabia and directly engaged the Iraqi troops entrenched in Kuwait. Unknown to the Iraqi troops, another force entered the great Syrian Desert and emerged behind the entrenched forces, making a 'left hook' manoeuvre. They liberated Kuwait in less than 100 hours and the war was over.

Had the Tomahawk not been fielded, the war would have been very difficult for the coalition forces due to prolonged conflict and loss of lives in greater numbers. The effectiveness of the Tomahawk class of cruise missiles was understood and it has since become a first-strike weapon.

As we set out to develop the 'fastest missile', we realized that it had to be a supersonic missile capable of travelling at speeds nearing Mach 3. We carried out a meticulous study on the systems that would be required – for example, the type of guidance system, the required airframe, and the type of engine for attaining supersonic speed. Alongside we analyzed the available expertise and the future expertise that we would need to develop the required systems for the missile.

We were confident about improving the guidance system of Prithvi missile for better accuracy and faster reaction time. Similarly, we were confident about developing the airframe. On the other hand, though, the engine had to be of a completely different class. It had to be an engineering marvel, something that had not been developed before. So, in theory it was a ramjet engine that ran on liquid fuel and had the necessary features to propel the missile to a speed of the order of Mach 3. We did wonder why nobody else had the supersonic cruise missile. Fighter aircraft flying at supersonic speed were operational but development of an engine for missile application was a real challenge. At that time, we were concentrating on developing a solid-fuelled ramjet engine for Akash missiles. We needed a ramjet engine whose technology had to be a derivative of the basic jet engine. But even for developing jet engines (aircraft) there was a total blackout in technology and expertise. This incompetence became a roadblock. Developing a ramjet engine at that point of time was itself a major programme that would take at least 10 years.

The goal of IGMDP was to achieve self-sufficiency in missile technology, eliminating the possibility of buying the engine off the shelf—supposing the engine existed in the first place. Yet, while the principles of IGMDP restricted buying, it did not prevent collaboration with another country possessing the ramjet engine technology. So, which nation would come forward to collaborate with us and what would be the win-win factor for both countries?

ISRO Days: Memories of France

In the 1970s, I was working in ISRO with Dr Kalam for the SLV-3 programme. We were based at Thiruvananthapuram. One day, Dr Sarabhai brought one visitor from France. He was Dr Curien, president of Centre Nationale de Etudes Spatiales (CNES), the French space research agency. Dr Curien and Dr Sarabhai helped to address some issues in the design of the fourth stage of SLV-3, for which Dr Kalam was the project manager.

Dr Curien then enquired whether the fourth stage of SLV-3 might be utilized for the Diamont rocket that they were developing. Dr Sarabhai who was witnessing the conversation had a beam of satisfaction on his face. Dr Curien's enquiry was nothing short of an accreditation for an 'infant space programme'. Unfortunately, the French cancelled the Diamont programme and communicated that our design was not required.

Some years later, France was designing a new launch vehicle called Ariane. You might have read in the newspapers about the INSAT being successfully stationed in the orbit by an Ariane rocket launched from Kourouin French Guiana. The Ariane rocket is a real workhorse of France and has placed a number of satellites in orbits.

Ariane was propelled by an engine called Viking. In 1974, ISRO and CNES signed an agreement for the transfer of Viking engine technology. ISRO scientists were allowed to work in the French propulsion-systems lab Société Européenne de Propulsion (SEP). The agreement required ISRO to provide 100 man-years to develop a version of Viking engine; this would allow them to receive the engine technology. France at that time badly needed a highly trained and knowledgeable workforce to quickly complete their Ariane programme. Their deadlines were crucial. The Indian scientists who worked there absorbed the technology within five years. Not only did they attain the 'know how', they also understood the 'know why'. By the time they came back to India, they had mastered the engine technology with which our engine Vikas was eventually developed. Today, it is Vikas that propels our PSLV and GSLV rockets.

Indo–Russian Relationship

Towards the end of 1955, Soviet leaders Nikita Khrushchev and Nikolai Bulganin visited India, marking the beginning of a long-standing relationship between the two countries. The then USSR diplomatically supported India during the wars with China and Pakistan in 1962 and 1965, respectively. In 1971, when war clouds were looming over India and Pakistan, the Chinese expressed their support to Pakistan. The USA and Pakistan had strong ties and the latter was a member of Central Treaty Organization (CENTO) and Southeast Asia Treaty Organization (SEATO), both military pacts.

Against this backdrop, in August 1971 India and USSR signed an important agreement called 'Treaty of Peace, Friendship and Cooperation'. According to this treaty, when one of the two nations was at war, the other would render military support. The treaty emphasized mutual respect and sovereignty for each other irrespective of ideological differences. The treaty was legally valid for a period of 20 years. Because of this treaty, other countries did not have the nerve to intervene.

In Space Research

The Russian contribution in the development of Indian space research capabilities has been remarkable. India's first satellite Aryabhatta and the remote-sensing satellites Bhaskara-1 and Bhaskara-2 used launch vehicles of the Soviet Union. Our operational remote-sensing satellites IRS-1A, IRS-1B and IRS-1C were also launched through Soviet launch vehicles.

In the early 1980s, a joint manned space programme was planned by ISRO and the Soviet Union's Intercosmos. Three cosmonauts – Yuri Malyshev, Gennadi Strekalov from Russia and Rakesh Sharma from India – were selected for the programme. On 3 April 1984, the Soviet

> Over and above everything was perhaps the goodwill between the two nations. After the 1971 war, the USSR had earned itself a special place in the minds of Indians. Whenever a Soviet leader or a Soviet citizen visited India, they were welcomed wholeheartedly by the people of India. Soviet achievers like Valentina Tereshkova (first female cosmonaut to reach space), Yury Gagarin (first cosmonaut to reach space) and Sergey Bubka (famous pole vault athlete) became household names.
>
> During our initial negotiation phase for BrahMos, we were in Russia. We were travelling in a metro. A man who was sitting on the opposite seat saw us and with a smile asked, "Raj Kapoor?" He mentioned the famous Indian actor. We were startled and later came to know that Russians were great fans of Raj Kapoor. He talked with bitterness about the breakup of Soviet Union and the lost glory. When it was time for him to get down at the station, he wished us good luck and said, "Indians are our friends and will always be."

launch vehicle Soyuz T-11 took off from the Baikonurcosmodrome to Salyut-7, a low Earth orbit space station. The crew spent a total of 7 days, 21 hours and 40 minutes in space aboard Salyut-7, conducting an earth observation programme concentrating on India. The then prime minister of India Mrs Indira Gandhi asked Sharma during a teleconference, "How is India looking like?" Sharma answered, "Saarejahanse achcha" (better than all lands). He made millions of Indians proud.

The next major cooperation was on the cryogenic engine for the Geosynchronous Satellite Launch Vehicle (GSLV) at its third stage. The agreement to develop an engine in India based on Russian design was stopped by the US, making it a MTCR issue. Subsequently, ISRO successfully developed its own cryogenic engine for future flights.

In Economic Development

The economic cooperation between the then USSR and India goes back to the early Fifties. Initially it came as Soviet help for the Bhilai steel plant, one of the first of its kind in India. This installation helped to kick-start the iron and steel industry in India. Similarly, considerable aid was provided by the USSR for the Indian Institute of Technology, Bombay. Soviet cooperation was extended over many strategic civilian production areas like heavy engineering machinery, oil exploration and refining, coal mining and power generation, etc. This initial boost in due course led India to become self-sufficient in the concerned areas.

In Arms Trade

The USSR and then later the Russian Federation has been our major source in procuring weapon platforms when no other nation was willing to sell to us. Many weapon systems were sold to us on loan with cheap interests or at a friendly price. Among the modern systems that India availed of were the Sukhoi-30 MKI aircraft with many western avionics. Also, six state-of-the-art stealth frigates called Talwar class were constructed for the Indian Navy at the Yantar shipyard at Kaliningrad. Also, as a gesture of friendship, a nuclear-powered submarine was leased to India.

Integrated Long Term Programme (ILTP)

During the World Wars and later during the Cold War period, Russia had established many design bureaus that supported the military-industry complex with research-and-development effort in high technology areas. Over a period, Russia had a knowledge pool at different establishments looking for opportunities to carryout research in newer areas. India and Russia decided to introduce the Integrated Long-Term Programme (ILTP) to enable continuation of research work and sharing of knowledge. DRDO utilized this opportunity and formed a joint R&D group for initiating research cooperation in selected areas and for providing consultancy in complex technology development projects. Many civilian, space and military projects have benefited from such cooperation.

One of the leading design bureaus in Russia was NPO Mashinostroyenia (NPOM), which specialized in launch vehicle and cruise missile technologies. As the other half of the BrahMos alliance, the illustrious journey of NPOM merits a separate section.

5

NPOM: VENTURE PARTNER

NPOM is the acronym for Naochno Proezvodsvyenoye Obyedeenyeneeye Mashinostroyenia (Scientific and Production Machine Building Association). One of the leading space and rocketry companies of Russia, NPOMhas accomplished more than 50 large-scale missile and rocket programmes. NPOM has also been engaged in three national defence programmes: arming the Soviet/Russian Navy with cruise missile complexes capable of being launched from surface, underwater and land-based platforms; arming the strategic nuclear forces with intercontinental ballistic missiles; and development of space systems and spacecraft, and automatic and manned orbital stations. NPOM has been a specialist organization for cruise missiles. In fact, around 60 per cent–70 per cent of the cruise missiles that are being operated by the Russian Navy have been designed and developed by NPOM.

Now an open joint-stock company, NPOM was set up as a design bureau in 1944 by the legendary scientist and engineer Vladimir Nikolaevich Chelomey. We will briefly look into the interesting history of Chelomey and his association with NPOM.

Chelomey was born during WWI. After his doctoral research, in Moscow he was concentrating on pulsating jet engines and related dynamics problems. WWII was in full swing and Hitler was creating havoc with his V-1 missiles barrage against London. After great difficulty the Britons equipped themselves to shoot down the V-1. Since Britain was an ally of the USSR during WWII, some of the remains of V-1 were sent to Moscow.

In 1944, Chelomey was asked to reverse-engineer the German weapon. He was a visionary and had rightly understood the potential of cruise missiles. Soon he was appointed as chief designer of Aviation Plant No. 51. By the middle of 1945 he had designed the first cruise missile of the USSR. Though it was just a copy and not produced in mass, it definitely marked the beginning of cruise missiles in his country.

Chelomey proposed to the Soviet Air Force improved versions of his air-launched cruise missiles (the flying bombs such as 10X, 12X, 14X and 16X) to be launched from long-range bombers. A Special Design Group (SKG-10) was created in the town of Tushino near Moscow, from where Chelomey started promoting his winged missiles for naval use, particularly for submarines. The Soviet Navy was also interested in such projects, as the Soviet strategy was to counter the aircraft carrier-based Western naval doctrine with submarines equipped with missiles.

In 1955, the SKG-10 was reinvented as Opitno Konstroktorskogo Bureau-52 (meaning Experimental Design Bureau-52),or simply OKB-52. In the post-WWII era, aircraft carriers became the principal stay in naval power. The Cold War between the USSR and the West had started. Attack against the USSR by NATO aircraft taking off from aircraft carriers was perceived as a significant threat. The USSR was trying to identify a suitable weapon – a deterrent against the naval threat. The weapon was supposed to have long-range, higher hit accuracy with ample destructive effect, be efficient in flight manoeuvres, and be operationally capable during all weather conditions.

After various analyses, cruise missiles launched from surface ships – and especially from submarines – were identified as possessing all the desired characteristics. Initially, cruise missiles launched from submarines were given the role of land attack with a nuclear payload, while anti-ship attack was considered secondary. Changes in the Soviet policy and the need for cruise missiles were felt in the early Fifties and by this time NPOM was established as OKB-52.

With his hands-on experience gained during the development of the 10X-series air-launched cruise missiles, Chelomey took part in a competition for the design of the new cruise missile. His design was ingenious and revolutionary and included the missile's wings being folded during storage. When the wings are folded, the body of the missile becomes almost cylindrical and can be stored in tubes, technically called canisters. When launched from a canister, the wings get unfolded in an ordered sequence in the air. Chelomey got this revolutionary idea by watching birds coming out of a small hole in the tree and spreading their wings the instant they came out. Ultimately, this design won the competition. From that moment, the folding wings and container-launched configuration became an inherent part of NPOM cruise missiles. This missile was named Project-5 and got inducted in the Soviet diesel electric submarines.

The missile's design was a pencil-shaped fuselage with swept wings and propelled by a turbojet engine with air intake under the belly. When launched, the missile used its rocket-assisted take-off (RATO) boosters for launch. After reaching the desired speed, the used boosters would jettison and the turbojet engine would start. This became a standard feature in all future NPOM cruise missiles. The P-5 had a range of 500 km and the guidance was based on autonomous inertial navigation system. Even with the limited accuracy of guidance systems at that time, the P-5 was usually armed with a nuclear warhead.

Immediately after induction, the same missile was equipped with a radar navigation unit and was named P-5D. By 1962 it was inducted in service for anti-shipping roles. The very same P-5D was also produced as a surface-to-surface missile complex for tactical use, as a coastal defence missile. This variant was called C-5. During the development process, the most complicated scientific-technical problems kept cropping up. Launching the missile from the container and the algorithm for designs of the wings' unfolding was too complex a job. A millisecond miss in synchronization would eventually lead to a catastrophe. Chelomey, himself being a professor, formed a close network with academia and NPOM and solved all the technical issues. Later, when a team from NPOM visited DRDO during the formation of the JV and they came to know about the networking of academia and industries for our IGMDP, they were highly impressed – that was Chelomey's style of working as well.

After the P-5 programmes, the Soviet Navy was relieved of the task of land attack and it was assigned to the strategic rocket forces, where Chelomey's contribution was already visible. By this time, NPOM was working on two anti-ship missile variants for dealing with Western aircraft-carrier task forces. One variant, P-35, was capable of being launched from surface ships and the other, P-6, could be launched from submarines. A land-based coastal-defence variant of P-35 was also developed. These missiles had INS-based navigation system and an active Doppler radar-based guidance for the terminal attack sequence.

The missile was way ahead of its predecessors in terms of both technology and capability. But it still required the submarine to stay on the water surface – its weakest attribute. So a new missile, the Ametist, was conceived – it had to be capable of being launched from a submarine, in submerged stage. Eventually, this missile became the world's first cruise missile capable of being launched from a submerged submarine. Now the Soviet Union was far ahead—at least by a decade—in comparison to the West.

The Ametist was followed by an improved missile, the Malakhit. This one had multiple-launch capability, meaning it could be launched from a submerged submarine as well as from a surface ship. The Malakhit possessed longer-range, improved guidance systems and was loaded with a superior flight profile compared to its predecessors. It had a range of around 70 km from a submarine and 110 km from a surface vessel. It could carry 500 kg explosive warhead or a nuclear warhead and fly at a speed of 0.9 Mach. Eventually, this missile was inducted in the Soviet Navy in the early 1970s.

After these missiles, NPOM began to develop a new missile complex – it was called P-500 Bazalt. This was a replacement for the P-6 and P-35 missiles and had a greater range and speed with improved flight characteristics. This missile became the first cruise missile capable of travelling at a supersonic speed of Mach 2. It was inducted in the late Seventies and early Eighties.

During the days of designing the Ametist and the Malakhit missiles, Chelomey concluded that it was necessary to design long-range missiles with universal launch capabilities. This line of thought resulted in a new missile called P-700 Granit, designed in the early 1970s to replace the Ametist and the Malakhit. But to fit the bill, the missile needed a robust system that could provide information about targets. This requirement could be met only through sea surveillance satellites and hence Chelomey began to develop such a system. It was assumed that sea surveillance satellites would be brought to the orbit by launch vehicles developed by NPOM. The additional role of this launch vehicle was to deliver the world's first manoeuvrable satellite to space, and its development was underway at NPOM. The launch vehicle was developed and designated as UR-200.

NPOM and Space Vehicles

When manned space programme was conceived in the USSR, a launch vehicle weighing around 500 tonnes was needed. NPOM had designed and developed a launch vehicle, UR-500, in the 1960s. This experience allowed NPOM to design a launch vehicle, Proton, for the Soviet lunar programme. The Proton created history by ensuring successful launches of many manned space stations (like the Salut family) and automated stations (like Almaz, Venus, Zond, Luna and Mars). These sections formed the basic compartment and other modules of the famous Mir complex. The versatility of UR-500 and another launch vehicle called UR-200 allowed them to be used as ballistic missiles as well.

These experiences led to the development and commissioning of the canisterized intercontinental ballistic missile UR-100. Till the middle of the 1980s, NPOM developed and put into service several versions of missile complexes with ICBM of this class (UR-100K, UR-100Y, UR-100N, UR-100N U TTX). NPOM has been a dynamic organization with specialization in cruise missiles and space vehicle development. They always started a new and ambitious project when another project was nearing completion.

Now they wanted to develop a new cruise missile for the Russian Naval Fleet which could be launched from underwater as well as from the surface as an anti-ship missile. Previously, all the cruise missiles of NPOM had turbojet propulsion due to which they could only attain subsonic speed. They envisioned that the new missile would be designed with a ramjet engine based on liquid fuel – a quantum leap from the previous missiles. NPOM eventually succeeded in the development of a unique ramjet engine, the equivalent of which did not exist anywhere in the world. NPOM conducted several ground and flight tests to check the engine of the supersonic anti-ship cruise missile. Unfortunately, the disintegration of the Soviet Union in the early 1990s affected the economy of the Russian Federation, ultimately bringing all research and development projects to a halt. For NPOM, the negation of its project at the completion stage was a near-fatal blow.

6

A JV IN THE MAKING

In India, we were in the process of identifying various technologies required for the realization of a supersonic cruise missile. We were open to collaborating in advanced technologies so that the development time could be minimized. So, when we came to know about NPOM's efforts, it seemed to us that a partnership might be in the offing there.

The formation of the joint venture itself was a long-winded process. The number of man-hours spent in negotiations and discussions, and the amount of paper communication that were carried out were countless. This single story of establishing the JV company against all odds can be written as a separate book. Here I present it in a nutshell.

AN ANONYMOUS COMPANY

To start with, developing the BRAHMOS missile was a top-secret programme. On 5 December 1995, a company was registered as BrahMos Private Limited in Delhi. All the formalities were completed in the ministry of company affairs. Even in that office, nobody knew what this company was made for. The Indian economy was looking up and several first-generation entrepreneurs had started their businesses. So this newly formed company was just another one among hundreds of registered private companies.

In the early Nineties, the USSR was officially dissolved and the Russian

Federation emerged as the successor nation. Those were years of trouble for both India and Russia. Russia was badly affected by the financial crisis brought about by the sudden dissolution. Geopolitically, India suffered due to a lack of strong friends. Her defence forces too suffered for lack of spares for their weapon platforms since nearly 90 per cent of them were of Soviet origin. Many of the defence industries that were situated all over the Soviet Union went along with the break away nations. During those difficult times, DRDO helped many Russian design bureaus to continue their R&D projects so that the scientific talent could be preserved and the exodus of the scientists controlled. I was heading the R&D group from the Indian side to maintain the collaborative efforts.

During one assignment at Moscow, I was discussing with our Russian friends the outcome of the Persian Gulf War. The conversation slowly moved towards the conduct of the war and the usage of air power. Inevitably, the focus shifted towards the Tomahawk and the role played by it. I expressed my wish that India too should have a cruise missile – one that was superior to the Tomahawk. The NPOM team got interested and the discussion turned towards our search for a liquid ramjet engine. A quick, barely audible discussion ensued among the NPOM team members. One of the members said that they already possessed a fully developed liquid ramjet engine that could give supersonic speed. Then he narrated the story of their cruise missile development programmes and spoke about Dr Chelomey's contributions. They had test-flown a prototype missile with the liquid ramjet engine but refused to divulge any more information. He regretted that they could not continue the programme due to the severe economic crisis.

I pondered over this discussion for many days after coming back to India. In my next visit to NPOM in 1993, I met the then director-general Dr Yefremov. He recalled the development effort put in by NPOM in developing the supersonic engine. He disclosed that the Germans wanted to acquire the technology from Russia but the latter did not reciprocate. However, with regard to India, it would be possible for Russia to agree to technology transfer and produce these engines in India. This would enable India to not only manufacture the engines but also configure a supersonic cruise missile. He then asked Mr Strakhov and Mr Khomyakov to show the engine to me and explain its significance. I was taken to a hangar in the afternoon to see the engine, which was covered like all the other things there so that the secrecy was maintained. When I heard the explanation about the engine, I realized its importance all the more.

Dr Yefremov continued the discussions with Mr R Ramanathan, the then additional financial advisor at DRDO, and Vice Admiral (Retd) Bharat Bhushan, who was the director-general of Advanced Technology Vehicle Programme (ATVP) when they visited NPOM. Based on these discussions, Mr Ramanathan generated a note (an official communication) on the possibility of transfer of technology of the engine and the need to involve a team for details. Further deliberations led to the idea of forming a collaborative effort to design and develop a supersonic cruise missile. A joint feasibility study team was set up: Mr Ramanathan, Mr Venugopalanand were from DRDO, and from NPOM the members were Dr Leonov, who is the present director-general of NPOM, Mr Strakhov and Mr Khromoshkin.

During their deliberations the team found that the supersonic engine could be used with a particular configuration for the missile. Further, substantial inputs were available for developing a supersonic cruise missile if the technological assets from both countries were brought to complement each other. We discussed the above details with Mr Ronen Sen, the then Indian ambassador at Russia. He suggested the possibility of a joint venture. He then wrote a letter to Dr Kalam advising him to work out the joint venture format with independent status. The scope of the committee was then modified to study the setting up of a joint venture to design, develop, manufacture and market the advanced missile.

Preliminary analysis of the proceedings of the joint committee resulted in generating a proposal from DRDO to the Government of India recommending a joint venture concept and seeking in-principle approval. Mr PV Narasimha Rao, the then prime minister who was also the defence minister, reviewed the proposal and approved the idea of a joint venture.

The three-member team comprising Ramanathan, Venugopalan and myself were assessing the formation of the joint venture, particularly in the context of the Soviet Union disintegrating into a number of countries. NPOM was not in a position to talk of share capital as Russia was gripped by a tough and adverse economical situation. They proposed that they would provide knowledge and technology, with their share to be valued at 50 per cent of the total capital. The remaining 50 per cent required for the full development would come as hot currency from the Indian Government. The original estimate for the joint venture was $1,500 million, which meant India had to contribute $750 million. This was not accepted by the Indian side. Detailed analyses and India's insistence over Russian contribution in cash led to scheduling of several meetings of the committee and the work progressed slowly. A tremendous amount of perseverance and frequent visits to Russia finally led the committee to settle the amount at $250 million for the development effort of a shore-based anti-ship missile complex.

NPOM discussed the issue with the Russian Government and coaxed them to address the financial problems. One has to remember that the political climate at the time was not conducive and the Government was not sufficiently stable to arrive at a concrete decision regarding such policies. Here, I have all the praise for Dr Yefremov and his tireless efforts to get approval for the JV company from the Russian Government. The Russian Government appointed a specialist committee to review the capabilities and technical competencies of DRDO to enter into a joint venture. At DRDO, we selected specific establishments to showcase the technological competence and milestones achieved. The Russian specialist committee led by Mr Sepnov, head of Russian Military Industries, and Dr Yefremov made a visit to DRDO establishments at Delhi, Dehradun, Hyderabad and Bangalore. The Russian specialists were awestruck and very happy on seeing our capabilities, especially in missile technology, guidance and control, software packages, computing capabilities and electronics systems. The specialist committee went back satisfied and their report suggested that DRDO was the right partner for the JV company.

However, NPOM's financial capacity was a concern. They were still not able to arrange funds for the JV company. Now they insisted that their process stock in terms of liquid ramjet engine, advanced booster, seeker, design knowledge and expertise be taken as share capital from their side as they had spent a huge amount to develop these technologies. Moreover, in the prevailing economic situation, there was no money available. Mr Ramanathan had a firm view that a joint venture could be formed only if both sides contributed money in cash as investment. Consequently, the two parties were staring at a stalemate.

We were discussing at the embassy with Mr Lambah, who had succeeded Mr Ronen Sen as ambassador. He said that the debt repayment being made by India to Russia every year for the credit could be converted into share capital from the Russian side. This audacious idea took everybody by surprise. Of course, it would be necessary for both governments to agree that repayment in kind by India be converted into cash and invested back in India. Mr Ramanathan and I effectively canvassed this idea to the Indian side. After several discussions in the finance ministry and Reserve Bank of India, we could see a light of hope from the Indian side. The big question was whether the finance experts from Russia would agree.

After finding a way of calculating the money India had to pay against the debts to Russia, Mr Ramanathan and I went to the Russian finance ministry along with Mr Khromoushkin and Mr Semaev, the representatives of NPOM. There, we met a lady who was a top Russian bureaucrat and presented the JV proposal to her. She was of typical Russian built, clearly more than a foot taller than us, and had a very strong voice. Because of the presence of Ramanathan, I was confident that we would be able to manage the interaction well, as scientists and bureaucrats do not generally gel with each other.

She was puzzled by the proposal because of the tight grip of economic crisis over Russia. She asked us politely to clear the place, saying that Russia's financial conditions were not conducive for undertaking a JV. When we explained the part about conversion of the debt money into investment, she started laughing andsaid, "It used to be the Soviet Union but now it is Russian Federation. It was friendship then. Hence the rupee-rouble trade adjustments were made. But now, for any partnership the dollar is the currency. How is it possible for me to take the debt money as investment?"

We were a bit taken aback and discussed the issue with the ambassador Mr Lambah. Mr Lambah handled the financing issues remarkably well. He took me to Mr Kudrin, the then Russian deputy minister for finance. Mr Kudrin avowed his support for the project then and there. He believed that the success of the joint venture would be a way out of the economic turmoil. After getting the nod from him, the ambassador asked me to meet the lady who was incharge of financial arrangements from the Russian side – as it turned out, the same top bureaucrat at the Russian finance ministry whom I had already met.

Again, Ramanathan and I knocked at the doors of the lady's office and conveyed the news that the deputy minister for finance had agreed to the JV. This time too, she gave us the cold shoulder stating that she had no instructions from the ministry and she was not open to any further discussion. So we returned.

A few weeks later, Dr Yefremov met the deputy minister for finance, following which the necessary instructions were given to the ministry officials. I again met the lady official in the finance ministry, knowing well that she had got all the directions. When I approached her this time, she was very friendly and informed that she was making a document exploring the possibilities for a JV. In truth, she had no opposition to the proposal but was a staunch follower of rules and instructions. Once she got the green signal, she extended all cooperation towards the project. The proposal was finally sent to the then president of the Russian Federation Mr Yeltsin.

The proposal for a joint venture was discussed between the governments of the Russian Federation and India. The idea of the two governments was to form a JV with three shareholders: DRDO (49 per cent), NPOM (49 per cent) and an Indian financial institution (2 per cent). This would provide equal partnerships to DRDO and NPOM and at the same time make it an overall 51 per cent for India, allowing the JV company to be instituted in India. Also, with 49 per cent for DRDO, the JV will become a private sector company. The concept of a private sector company was agreed to by both the governments in order to give it flexibility and freedom from the regulations of both governments in day-to-day affairs.

Now, identifying a third partner became an issue since the joint venture was classified as a top-secret project. There were concerns that inclusion of a financial institution may compromise the secrecy. It was proposed that only DRDO and NPOM be the partners, holding 51 per cent and 49 per cent respectively. Mr Ahluwalia, the finance secretary, reviewed the proposal and raised the point that this ratio might result in the JV losing the advantage of private sector status. (In India, when the government share is 51 per cent, the company will be a public sector undertaking [PSU], like Hindustan Aeronautics Limited [HAL].) This would place the JV company under the direct control of the Indian defence ministry, which was not acceptable to the Russian side. They feared that procedural formalities and government controls from the Indian side would delay the operations of the joint venture. So the best way to tackle this difficulty was to make the company a private sector with less than 51 per cent for the Indian side. The Russian side demanded equal partnership and control in the operations of the company. In a novel way, we did just that with a new share percentage of 50.5 per cent for DRDO and 49.5 per cent for NPOM.

Dr Kalam, Ramanathan and I presented the funding pattern for the joint venture to Mr PV Narasimha Rao. He went through the intricacies of the formation of the joint venture, the financing scheme, and asked a few questions accompanied with his usual facial gesture, which could not be understood by anyone. Finally he nodded his head and said, "It is a good idea and if it clicks it has a great future." The political will exhibited by him gave us tremendous confidence. At last, the BrahMos JV was registered on 5 December 1995 at Registrar of Companies in New Delhi. The approval from the Russian side was yet to come, though.

The years 1996 and 1997 saw much political turmoil in Russia. Hence, the proposal had to go through many hands again and again due to which we lost two very valuable years. Mr Pukhamov, the then deputy minister of defence in Russia, and finalized the draft of the Inter Governmental Agreement (IGA) with the participation of the NPOM team. Finally, we got the decree issued by the president of the Russian Federation permitting the JV. On 12 February 1998, the IGA was signed in Moscow by Dr Kalam on behalf of Government of India and Deputy Minister of Defence Mr NV Michaelovon behalf of Russian Government.

Again, after a series of persuasion, on 12 August 1998 the Russian Government issued a decree on the modality of financing the JV. The presidential decree accepted the conversion of loan money owed by India as the Russian contribution for capital money. On 23 March 1999, the Inter Government 'Memorandum on Financing of JV' was signed by Mr Lambah on behalf of Government of India. According to the agreement,

India and Russia would jointly contribute 250 million dollars to the project at the ratio of 50.5 per cent and 49.5 per cent.

Overall, BrahMos came into existence because of the deep professional rapport and trust among the key persons. Dr Kalam and Dr Yefremov believed in each other and their team of experts. Not once did Dr Kalam reject any proposal of mine. Similarly, whenever Dr Kalam forwarded a proposal to Mr Narasimha Rao, it usually came back on the same day with his approval. A similar rapport existed between Ramanathan, the then financial advisor (defence services) Mr Sivasubramanian, Dr Kalam and me. So proposals sailed forward with quick winds in the bureaucratic channels.

On the Russian side, the academic stature of Dr Yefremov and his legendary role as missile designer helped to move things faster. His name and stature was able to get many things done in Russia. This I have seen with my own eyes.

On 8 July 1999, the company BrahMos was officially operational with funding. On the very next day, a tripartite agreement was signed between DRDO, NPOM and BrahMos, with Dr Kalam, Dr Yefremov and I respectively sharing the responsibilities for the three organizations. This agreement was yet another novel modality where the shareholders themselves became the contractors for the job to be done. By that agreement, BrahMos,a private company, gave contracts to DRDO and NPOM to develop certain systems. DRDO was to develop and provide the guidance components, airframe and launcher systems for flight testing. NPOM was to provide the liquid engine, booster and seeker for flight tests.

We did not sit idle during the intervening period of more than three years from registration to operationalization of the company. Before we were able to get funds, we were conducting periodical meetings and basic design works through the staff seconded to the company by the parent organizations. So, when we received the funds we were ready with our designs, modalities, schedules and even marketing strategies. For us, marketing strategies were not confined to the domestic market (Indian and Russian armed forces); we took into account the international market as well. Those three years were really the formative years for the company.

7

Moving Ahead

The new company could not be situated in the premises of DRDO; it had to have a secluded place with adequate security. Our Russian partners had to come for meetings and some would stay to work with us. Everyday would be buzzing with activities. These movements were not supposed to attract the attention of people around because of the nature of our project. We rented a building in Vasant Vihar, a residential locality in Delhi, with 10 employees initially. The locality had many foreign embassies and that gave us a perfect cover for the visiting foreigners. People considered the office as a sort of an embassy. There was no signboard for the office and even today we don't have any!

The board of directors had been formed; but just directors could not run the day-to-day activities of an organization. We had to hire employees, but how? We gave an advertisement in the newspapers: 'A leading MNC needs personnel for the following vacancies... those interested may walk in.' Thousands of people must have seen this advertisement and thought which MNC would advertise without revealing their name. So it was that only a very few came forward for the interview. The venue for the interview was an apartment that operated as a DRDO guesthouse. Many walked away even before the interview. Those who were selected were intimated through telephone to arrive at a particular address for taking charge. No letters were issued. Some of the selected ones felt that the company was bogus and left even before taking charge. As for those who took charge, they found it incredible that they were going to take part in India's top-secret missile development programme. Some of the newcomers from that time hold prestigious posts in the company today.

Everybody was given a specific work with separate instructions. One person's work was not to be known to the other. This was to reduce the flow of information and to plug the information leak. For example, an employee would be asked to draft an important and secret communication without their counterpart knowing. Another employee would be sent somewhere and was not available in the office for many days. The others knew not to enquire about their absence, nor did that particular person revealed where they had been.

As in other companies, we had a front office management system but the staff never revealed anything about the company to callers. Unknown calls were not entertained. When calls were made from our office to other offices, even if they were government ones, our identity was not disclosed. The norms were so strict that no government vehicles were used in our day-to-day operations.

An important identifier for any company is its logo; standard company communications are made through the company letterhead. To maintain secrecy we did not use any. All our communications had the word BrahMos, and that was all. The office that we had rented was a bungalow. We used the servant quarters as rooms for the staff and the underground cellar served as our library and conference room. We undertook welding of all the windows so that they could not be opened. We had to eliminate all possibilities of theft. There were computers with critical data. For us, the data going into anybody else's hand meant that the secrecy was over. So we had to take such extreme precautions.

At the laboratory level, the R&D work was simultaneously being carried out at both NPOM and DRDL. Instead of using the word BrahMos, a code name – PJ-10 – was created. This secrecy was maintained until the first flight trial. Only after that the name BrahMos shared with the media for the first time.

Giving an Identity

The JV Company has to be given an identity. What are the identities of a company? It has a name and a logo. We needed them. But getting them was a strange experience and that too through strange process.

Naming the Company

After the Indian Government approved the joint venture, the core group from DRDO and a team from NPOM headed by Dr Yefremov got together to coin a name. Water as a metaphor and as a vital resource for life came to our minds. One of the five elements of nature, water is a wonderful lesson in vibrancy. An organization will be healthy only when it is vibrant. The vibrancy of an organization lies in its thirst to grow through a progressive vision of the future. The thirst for growth leads the organization to scale summits and venture into deeper oceans.

The fury of the water in the Brahmaputra, the mightiest river of India bearing the name of Brahma the creator, is a source of inspiration and vibrancy. The Neva is a mighty river in Russia. Both the teams were looking for a combination of the names of the two rivers. NPOM suggested the river Moskva as the Russian identity, as NPOM was situated near the bank of the Moskva. We tried various combinations and finally as arrived at BRAHMA-MOSKOVA, resulting in BrahMos – combining the fury of the Brahmaputra and the grace of the Moskva. I was happily thinking of the coincidence that the name of the celestial weapon created by Lord Brahma, known as the Brahmastra, was now given to our missile. All in NPOM were convinced with the name due to the historic background of the two rivers one at the feet of goddess Shakti at Guwahati (Assam) in the eastern India and the other flowing near the seat of power - Kremlin. Eventually, the company was named as BrahMos and later renamed as BrahMos Aerospace. In the later years, we christened the missile as BRAHMOS.

The Symbol

The logo for the company had to reflect the theme and purpose. National Institute of Design (NID) in Ahmedabad was given the task of designing the logo. Of the several options, one was chosen to highlight the following:

- The mighty forces of the two rivers and the two great countries joined together to create the power that was equivalent to the Shiv Ling
- Two lines symbolizing the two organizations DRDO and NPOM with their varying capabilities, cultures, languages, aspirations coming together to carry on one project, representing speed.

SYMBOLIC CONTRIBUTION OF PARTNERS – IDOLS OF POWER AND PRECISION

I narrated about the depiction of the name BrahMos in the atrium in the form of mosaic. The thought came to my mind why can't the prime qualities of our missile be depicted inside the building. The construction of the building itself is separated into two wings. An idea came to my mind that since our product is a Weapon i.e. Missile and the upper portion of side walls at the left wing can be carved with the scenes of the mighty Astras (Weapons) being used in the great war of Mahabharata – An Indian Epic. At the same time, at the centre of the wing, we have constructed a sculpture denoting a scene from Mahabharata, where Arjuna aims at a fish rotating above, by just looking at the reflection of that fish in the water below signifying the precision of the missile which is provided by the Indian guidance system. Similarly, in the right wing of the building, the upper portion of side walls is carved with the scenarios depicting great wars which the Russians had fought. Like the statue of Arjuna, the sculptors of medieval legendary Russian Warriors Ilya Muromets, Dobrynya Nikititch and Alousha Popovitch who were famous for their physical strength have been erected. Their muscle power represents the Power of BRAHMOS derived from the Ramjet Propulsion. Whoever visits the BrahMos Headquarters complex never fails to appreciate the ideas of placing these statues in the premises.

PART 4

Gaining Momentum

"All one has to do is just look around, find what the world does not have, and then head towards inventing it."

– Thomas Alva Edison

Here we come to the BRAHMOS missile system and the force-multiplication effect it has provided to our armed forces. In a nutshell, the missile has rightfully earned its fame as 'the world leader among cruise missiles' through its characteristics and qualities. We are not going to stop there, of course; we will develop more and more new weapon systems through our self-found path. The momentum picks up now.

8

Designing the Missile

The Gulf War in 1991 gave a clear message that the first-level attack on the enemy had to be through cruise missiles with high-precision engagement. Our intention to possess an advanced cruise missile system was absolutely clear, but it was necessary to take the lead by developing a supersonic cruise missile in the least possible time. What would help us to leapfrog and minimize the time from drawing board to front-line deployment, while ensuring operational effectiveness of the product and customer delight? That was the question before us.

Through IGMDP we had established higher levels of capability in inertial navigation system (INS), on-board computer (OBC), avionics, software and mission management. Now we required a new engine capable of providing supersonic speed. We had the expertise in solid propellant ramjet engine technology, as demonstrated in the Akash project. For the long-range cruise missile and for its growth potential, the optimum choice was the liquid-fuelled ramjet engine, which was two times more energy-efficient compared to solid-fuelled ramjet. During our consultation with NPOMashinostroyenia for another project, Dr Yefremov, the Director General of NPOM was discussing with me on the possible future missions. He asked me to see their ramjet engine developed just before the breakup of Soviet Union. I was amazed to see the engine. After learning the specifications I realized that there was no equivalent available in the world.

It gave me a feeling of satisfaction that this engine could do miracles. Dr Yefremov immediately agreed that there was a strong possibility of collaboration in supersonic missile capability.

After assessing the overall characteristics of the engine, our team started looking at the shape of the missile. We realized that the combustion chamber of the engine could accommodate the booster. Thus, it would become a booster-sustainer combo, enabling us to reduce the length of the missile. Further discussions revealed that Russian experts had worked out a prototype configuration of the missile and conducted wind-tunnel tests on the model. NPOM had already carried out initial flight tests of the prototype to establish the propulsion system. The project could not progress further due to shortage of funds in the 1990s. It so happened, in Russia, that most of the design bureaus and R&D Centres started losing the best brains as they were moving out to other countries. Having worked with Russian specialists for many years, I felt it was a great loss if specialists leave the country at that critical juncture. A collaborative arrangement with NPOM for the cruise missile would help to retain the best manpower with them. Dr Yefremov was convinced with this fact.

The initial data on the design of the missile was discussed with the joint team. Further optimization studies were carried out incorporating Indian subsystems. Slowly, the supersonic BRAHMOS took shape. The universal characteristics of the missile for sea, sub-sea and land launch capabilities encouraged us to freeze the design for anti-ship application.

Now we had two options with us. One was to develop an entirely new airframe for the missile. The other was to use the already designed and flight-tested airframe. Developing a new airframe based on the existing ramjet modules was possible. But to save cost and time, it would be wiser to go into Phase I with Russian design and materials fabricated in Indian industry.

It was a strategic decision. We decided not to reinvent the wheel but to exploit and augment the missile's capability in a step-by-step process. Since the Russian missile was at a prototype stage, we were sure that its potential could be augmented with our contribution, especially for land-target engagement and warheads.

The next step was to design the guidance system. We took the state-of-the-art guidance system developed for Prithvi and improvised it. We augmented the accuracy of the guidance system and also reduced the reaction time.

As for the launcher systems, fire control systems, etc., we decided to develop state-of-the-art versions. Today, our land-based launcher systems are fully network-centric in operation and totally developed in India. There is no cruise missile system operating in the world along the lines of the land-attack version of the BRAHMOS, in the form of a universal missile.

In hindsight, it was the Indo–Russian partnership that worked well. Each side decided to respect the strength of the counterpart. Neither the Russian partners insisted on using their existing guidance systems nor did the Indian side insisted on developing their own airframe. It could have been done by both sides but abiding by the principle of 'strength respects strength', we combined the strengths of the two sides. Thus, the propulsion modules became the process stock of Russia and the guidance and on-board electronic modules became the process stock of India.

Multiple DRDO labs participated in the effort to realize the best design for India. A separate design team was formed to look at the suitable platform system like ship, submarine, road mobile complex and aircraft. The same missile could also be used against different types of targets so the developments of systems like Fire Control System and Launcher for the ship and land were started.

Time has proved our decision to be correct – a missile that was designed to be an anti-ship missile system has evolved into many fascinating versions capable of attacking targets that were earlier thought impossible. Thanks to the high-accuracy guidance system and high-power propulsion system, today we can even hit targets located in a valley.

This is nowhere near the end of it. BRAHMOS will be getting many new dimensions in the years to come. It will be capable of being launched from land platforms, aircraft and ships against sea and land targets in a salvo mode for fast and lethal deployment. Basically, it can be used on multiple platforms against multiple targets in multiple trajectories. The potential of BRAHMOS is huge. It is truly a Brahmastra!

BRAHMOS Unique Universal Missile

This approach resulted in the realization of one of the best designs for the Supersonic Cruise Missile which can be used in multiple platforms against multiple targets in multiple trajectories. What a great opportunity knocked on us to get into the development of fastest cruise missile! We carried out several development trials and saw successive success. Our each flight trial was really enterprising.

9

A Supersonic Bird

Alexander Vasilyevich Suvorov (1730–1800 CE) was the fourth generalissimo of the Russian Empire and regarded as one of the greatest generals of Russia. Had he been aware of the BRAHMOS, he would have reiterated that 'one second can decide the outcome of the battle'. So, what makes the BRAHMOS is superior and what are the features that make it a system par excellence?

The Others: A Capability Analysis

Cruise missiles are often classified as anti-ship cruise missile (ASCM) and land-attack cruise missile (LACM). From various estimates it has been concluded that around 75 nations in the world possess cruise missiles. Around 130 types of cruise missile are operational. An astonishing amount of 75,000 individual ASCMs exist all over the world. Overall there are 19 nations that produce such missiles. Among these 19, about 12 nations produce both LACMs and ASCMs and the remaining nations produce only ASCMs. The most popular missiles in the arms market include the US Harpoon; the Russian Uran and Klub; and the French Exocet.

With around 6,000 units having been sold, the US Harpoon is said to be the most sold missile. Next is the Exocet, 3,000 units of which are said to have been sold. Among Russian missiles, the Styx and its Chinese cousin, the HY-1 'silkworm', have been widely deployed. Russia is currently marketing the 3M-54 Klub family of missiles, which include the supersonic 3M-54E and the subsonic 3M-54E1 ASCMs as well as the 3M-14E LACM.

It is apparent that most of the missiles belong to the subsonic category. Aircraft, surface ships, submarines and land-based launchers are the four types of weapon platforms for launching these missiles. However, only a few of the missiles can be launched from all the four platforms.

The Harpoon (AGM-84), said to be the most sold missile, is predominantly an anti-ship missile and skims over the water surface with a radar guidance. Some land-attack variants also exist. These missiles can be launched from all the four weapon platforms.

The Exocet is famous for its anti-ship roles and has tasted blood several times, especially during the Falklands conflict. The missile can be launched from aircraft, surface ships and submarines; some land-based variants may exist.

The Kayak (AS-20) is a Russian missile whose air-launched variant is commonly referred to as the Uran. This missile is similar to the US Harpoon and has active radar guidance. It can be launched from all the four weapon platforms and even from helicopters.

The 3M-54 is a Russian missile and generally known as the Klub family of missiles. Three variants are for anti-ship role, two for anti-submarine role, and one for land-attack role. The anti-ship missile 3M-54E travels at a subsonic speed and when it is in the proximity of the ship, it fires another rocket that flies at a speed of 2.9 Mach.

The Moskit-E is another Russian ASCM that can be launched from surface vessel platform. It is a supersonic missile but the range is very limited – at 120 km, it is not even half the range of the BRAHMOS.

We have already discussed the Tomahawk. It is generally strategic in nature and can carry nuclear warheads for a fairly long range. In our analysis we have considered the Tomahawk to be a land-attack missile. It is the largely converted form of the Tomahawk anti-ship missiles that once existed. It flies by maintaining a constant altitude with respect to the ground and thus follows the terrain. If there is an elevation in the ground, the missile climbs up, and vice versa. Such missiles can be easily detected by the airborne warning and control systems (AWACS) aircraft with their huge radar. With a speed of just 0.7 Mach, it can be easily intercepted by fighter aircraft. The BRAHMOS with a speed of 2.9 Mach cannot be intercepted by any current fighter aircraft. In any case, considering the short flight time of the BRAHMOS, even if any aircraft were to try to engage it, the missile would have already accomplished its mission.

WHAT MAKES THE BRAHMOS SUPERIOR?

Well, It Is Supersonic

You may be wondering what the great advantage to being supersonic is. I will explain this aspect here.

The kinetic energy (KE) of the body is derived from its speed. Greater the speed, greater is the kinetic energy. Mathematically, the kinetic energy is:

$$KE = (mv^2)/2$$

So, the KE is half of the value derived by multiplying the mass (m) with the speed (v) squared. Through simple arithmetic we can see that if the speed is tripled then the resultant KE increases nine-fold.

Now BRAHMOS flies at a speed that is three times greater than the other missiles. So it impacts the target with energy roughly nine times greater than the other missiles. What is the benefit of the increased KE?

If the target ship is very huge or the target building is a hardened structure, the increased KE plays a crucial role. For knocking down a huge ship, two or three subsonic missiles may be required. But just one BRAHMOS missile will do the task of these two or three subsonic missiles.

The Speed Makes It Lethal

A need may arise to fly the BRAHMOS at a very low altitude in order to avoid detection by enemy radar. This type of trajectory is called 'flying on the nap of the earth'. As the earth is spherical, an airborne vehicle flying as though it is skimming over the ground cannot be detected from long distances through radars. The possibility of detection of the missile is near its target (for example, a ship). In case of ordinary missiles, the enemy gets a considerable amount of time to activate his defences. In case of BRAHMOS, as the speed is greater, the missile allows no time for the enemy to detect the incoming missile and act. As the speed is three times higher, the enemy's reaction time is reduced by one-third.

At the same time, the supersonic speed gives enormous kinetic energy to the missile – so, when it hits the target, it hits with a lethal force. In one of the flight trials, the target was a decommissioned ship. The missile penetrated the entire ship and went away; it was a sight to be seen. The damage caused was entirely due to the missile's speed.

It Can Hit Multiple Targets, and Precisely So

A single missile can hit a band of targets ranging from ships in the high seas to buildings deep inside the enemy land. The missile can hit vessels of various sizes, from small corvettes to large aircraft carriers. The user need not stock different missiles for different targets.

A missile can be faster and intelligent but in the war scenario what matters is the accuracy of the hit. The BRAHMOS missile has the highest accuracy rate among various missiles. In a war scenario, the accuracy of the hit matters as much as the missile's speed and intelligence.

Looking out for the Enemy

Assume that in pitch darkness you are supposed to find an enemy with a flashlight and he is also supposed to do the same. You can find the enemy using the flashlight and also without flashlight. How?

When your light is switched off, then there is only one light beam, which will be of the enemy. From that light beam you can find the location of the enemy's flashlight. The radar can be substituted for the flashlight as the radar also behaves exactly like a flashlight.

Detecting an enemy's presence by detecting his radar's emission is called electronic support measures (ESM). Once the enemy's position is detected, it becomes easy to confuse or counter him. Thus, when we have radar receivers, we can receive the enemy's radar signals and without using our radar actively, we can find out that the enemy is coming.

Often, a condition called emission control (EMCON) is imposed on the forces requiring them to stop emitting radar and communication signals. This was a lesson learnt during the Second World War. The Japanese had attacked the Americans at Pearl Harbour. The pilots had an instruction that after a certain distance they had to tune their radio receivers to the Pearl Harbour radio station's frequency. The unsuspecting Americans did not impose any restrictions on the broadcasting radio station (these signals are directional and we know this since radios in our homes receive well in one direction). Using these signals, the Japanese reached Pearl Harbour without much navigational hiccups and inflicted heavy damage.

Subsequently, all militaries learnt to reduce their signal emissions. They compensate this reduction by listening to the enemy signals. On detecting any emission, they initiate what is known as electronic counter-measure (ECM), whereby the enemy radar signals are confused and jammed.

The radar signals from the BRAHMOS do not attract the attention of enemy ESM systems.

It Can Follow MultipleTrajectories

The missile has been designed such that it can follow various trajectories and fly at various altitudes.

In high–low trajectory the missile climbs to a very high altitude. After maintaining the same course for a certain distance it dives sharply and follows the nap of the terrain. This trajectory is chiefly followed for anti-ship role as the missile approaches the target suddenly from the horizon and the enemy is then left with no solution except to say his final prayers.

A low–low trajectory is followed when the target is at a closer range. The missile will fly along the nap of the earth all through the entire flight. When the missile suddenly appears at the horizon, the enemy is left with no options.

A waypoint trajectory is followed when the enemy has

Low Radar Cross-Section

Radar cross-section (RCS) is a parameter that is used to indicate the reflectivity of an object to the radar. Generally, greater the surface area of a body, greater is the RCS, thus making it visible in radar precisely. A civilian transport aircraft reflects a lot moreradar energy back to the radar than a fighter aircraft and is highly visible in the radar. A cruise missile produces a RCS lesser than the fighter aircraft. Cruise missiles with deployable wings reflect a considerable amount of RCS. Since the BRAHMOS does not have deployable wings and is very compact, the missile does not produce much RCS. A lower RCS reduces the detection capability of the enemy radar. This makes the BRAHMOS inherently stealthy.

to be deceived. Through this trajectory the missile flies to the target through a different direction instead of the straight line. The missile can be directed to fly such that it circumvents an enemy air defence position that is expecting the missile. Presently the cruise missile defence systems are not capable enough to intercept BRAHMOS but they may be developed in the future. Even then, though, those systems can be cheated by using the waypoint manoeuvre. Assume that an enemy's sailing vessel is to be attacked. A salvo of four missiles can be launched with each missile to arrive at the vessel from all four directions. Each missile will fly at varied altitude so that the target vessel's defences will be overloaded with threats emanating from different directions in difference profiles. In case three missiles are intercepted, the fourth missile can still destroy the vessel.

In the steep-dive trajectory, the missile after reaching the target area dives vertically and hits the target over its head. This mode can be highly useful in hitting targets situated in mountains and partially buried command centres. No other missile in the world flies in a trajectory like this.

It Can Take off from Multiple Platforms

The BRAHMOS can be integrated with various weapon platforms like land-based launcher systems, surface vessels, aircraft and submarines. This means that the missile can be fired from land, air, sea and subsea platforms against targets on both land and sea, thus covering all layers of the war theatre. During a war, the enemy cannot predict from which platform the missile will be fired. Combining the multi-trajectory capability with the multiple-platform capability, the missile can strike the enemy from various directions and can bring him to his knees.

> The BRAHMOS can be launched vertically from a surface ship and horizontally from an aircraft. The maximum combat potential lies in a vertically launched missile where it has all the freedom to align itself with the target. The configuration of the BRAHMOS allows it to fit in all sorts of surface vessels and submarines. The capability to be launched from any angle makes the missile more robust for demanding combat environments.

In anti-ship missions, the missile has a very good range to hit a ship travelling in the deep seas. Such an advantage makes the missile a terrific weapon for coastal defence. Assume that our vessels are on patrol in the deep seas some 250 km away from the coast. When a fleet of enemy vessels is detected some 500 km away from the coast, the entire enemy fleet can be destroyed before they can launch any meaningful attack through their aircraft or missiles. Similarly, our missile can hit a coastal target by staying some 250 km well beyond in the international waters. Further, the missile can be launched from submarines, which can sneak near the enemy shore and then fire the missile.

In the 1971 war with Pakistan, our small coastal defence missile boats were taken up to the entrance of Karachi harbour to hit the enemy vessels and their installations. Those boats did not have the range and endurance to sail for longer distance. Hence they were towed to a very long distance off the coast of Bombay. Also, the missiles that were fired had a range of less than 80 km. Now, with the BRAHMOS, the naval vessels can stay in a standoff range, fire the missile against the enemy target and return.

The Indian Army has inducted the BRAHMOS missiles and these can be fired from a road-mobile vehicle. When a group of such vehicles are concentrated and they start firing the missiles, the enemy will see a volley of missiles. Just by staying well inside our territory our army can launch the missiles and may even end the war before it begins.

Work is underway to integrate the missiles with the Sukhoi-30 MKI aircraft of the IAF. When integrated with these aircraft, the missiles can be fired over a greater range with impunity, as these aircraft have enormous range. This makes the aircraft and the missile a deadly combination.

This Means It has Multi-Mission Capability

The BRAHMOS can perform various missions and it can fill the gap between the purely tactical missile and a strategic missile. In air war there are two types of bombing: strategic and tactical. In a nutshell, tactical bombing means bombing the weapon against platforms – like destroying ships, troops and tank columns. Strategic bombing means bombing the war-waging capability – like destroying factories, oil refineries, dams, etc. The BRAHMOS can be used to destroy both tactical and strategic targets since it can hit enemy vessels in the deep seas and also various strategic targets.

Moreover, the BRAHMOS has sophisticated electronic counter-countermeasures (ECCM) systems – these are both robust and jam-proof. Considering the supersonic speed of the missile, the ECM of the enemy cannot do any damage since the reaction time for him is very less.

It Can Do a Salvo

The missile is independent in nature – for example, two missiles with different targets can be launched from the same launching platform in quick succession. The two missiles in action do not interfere with each other. This feature enables multiple missiles to be launched either against a single target or against various targets. The INS *Ranvir* has eight missiles and all eight can be launched against eight different targets, that too in quick succession. Imagine a squadron of vessels or land-based launcher systems launching a volley of missiles to cripple the enemy even before he starts the war.

It is the Most Cost-Effective

When compared to other missiles, the BRAHMOS is much more economical in terms of capabilities and power. A single BRAHMOS missile can be used to destroy an important enemy installation like long-range radar, instead of sending a formation of aircraft. This reduces the risk for aircraft and pilots while operating inside enemy territory. At the same time, that formation can be used elsewhere – this means that an extra formation is available for combat duties. This is called force multiplying; a single missile provides the effect of a formation of aircraft.

The BRAHMOS versus a Typical Subsonic Cruise Missile

	Subsonic Cruise Missile	BRAHMOS
Speed	0.8 Mach	2.8 Mach
Time to hit the target	1 unit	1/3rd (faster engagement)
Kinetic energy	1 unit	9 times (high destructive power)
Target dispersion (moving targets)	1 unit	1/3rd (probability of hit is high)
Reaction time	1 unit	1/3rd (pierces the defence)
Universality	Nil	Same system for sea and land targets

It Lives Longer and is Easy on Maintenance

During production, the missile is assembled and inserted in a canister (cylinder). Like a scabbard protecting a sword, a canister protects the missile. This canister seals the missile in airtight condition. This ensures that the missile is safe from environmental degradation. In particular, the missile is well protected against oceanic corrosion while it is in warships.

Apart from being protected, the missile is easy to maintain. Usually, a lot of man-hours are spent to keep a sophisticated weapon system or platform in 'fighting fitness'. Some missiles may have to be tested once in a quarter, whereas BRAHMOS can be tested once in three years.

Sections of the Missile

Propulsion System

The propulsion system of the BRAHMOS missile is the most unique among any flying machine. This system can be described as a composite propulsion system as it contains a solid rocket booster and a ramjet sustainer. The ramjet engine can function only after attaining supersonic speed. So, to propel the missile to a required speed, a solid propellant-fuelled rocket booster is used. Solid propulsion systems are quick and do not need any tedious maintenance procedures. In many contemporary cruise missiles, the booster is attached to the exterior. In the BRAHMOS, the booster is housed inside the ramjet engine. However, the booster can become a hindrance for the ramjet engine as its additional weight remains of no use after its work is over. So the booster is jettisoned after the required speed is achieved. The space occupied by the booster becomes the combustion chamber of the ramjet engine. This makes the missile highly compact, allowing it to be stored inside the canister.

Nose Cap

The nose cap is used to seal the missile in the canister. It also protects the missile during underwater launches (that is, when launched from a submarine). Apart from the protection, it has combat utility. During vertical launches, it brings the missile to the proper course. To put it simply, it tilts the missile horizontally and orients the missile in the direction of the target, before the solid rocket booster fires. Suppose this feature is not available and the target is in another direction to the missile – in such a situation the missile will have to make a U-turn to reach the target. This will result in wastage of fuel, thereby reducing the range and eating into precious time. To avoid this, the nose cap twists the missile towards the target after it is ejected from the canister. Now the target will be right ahead of the missile and the nose cap works to tilt the missile to a horizontal position. After these manoeuvres, the nose cap itself becomes an unwanted load for the missile and hence gets ejected. The BRAHMOSis the only missile in the world that functions in an intelligent manner.

Target Seeker

The target seeker is basically a radar seeker. The seeker scans the area in front to find the target. An improved seeker has been developed for Block II version of the missile. This seeker will be used for the land-attack version of the missile for the army. (This is as per the requirement of the Indian Army to have a missile with target-discrimination capability – that is, the missile has to find and hit a specific target among a group of targets [for example, a specific building among a group of buildings].)

Airframe, Guidance and Control

The airframe of the missile is a perfect cylinder with small wings and fins. This design is critical for reducing the drag at supersonic speeds. Wings and fins are kept folded around the missile body inside the canister and when the missile leaves the canister they open up and get deployed. The wings are very small because even a small wing can provide sufficient lift at supersonic speeds. This is the reason why fighter aircraft have delta-shaped small wings, whereas airliners have huge wings. The smaller wing profile creates a negligible RCS, as I said earlier.

The wings are fixed and the fins move to turn the missile during the flight. There are four actuators to actuate the fins. These actuators are commanded by the guidance system.

The air intake for the ramjet engine is present in the nose of the missile. This also reduces the RCS. The annular fuel tank **is** shaped in such a way that the body of the missile itself acts as the wall for the fuel tank. The missile is very small in size when compared with the mechanical and electronic complications that are involved. The entire area is used for accommodating various subsystems and is a highly complex arrangement. Explaining further will make no sense as it is purely technical.

The guidance and control system is based on an INS that works in conjunction with an on-board computer (OBC). During the flight, the INS detects any deviation from the intended flight path and feeds the OBC, which then directs suitable aerodynamic features to restore the intended flight path. The target's coordinates are fed to the OBC via a fire control system (FCS) present in the launcher before launching the missile. The missile then flies to the target area by deriving inputs from the INS and the seeker.

Warhead

The warhead of the missile can store 200 kg of high explosive (HE) material. In one of the flight trials, we fired the missile with a live warhead. The missile flew and hit the target, a decommissioned naval vessel, and it sank within six minutes. When we went to inspect the target after the hit, there was no target – there were not even much debris. Likewise, when the same warhead is used against a land target like a building, only the debris will be left. Such effect is possible because the lethality of the warhead is augmented by the supersonic speed of the missile.

There are several other superior features in the missile and associated systems, but their secrecy has to be maintained for the sake of the nation's security.

10

Multi-Platform Capability

The strength of BRAHMOS missile is augmented through the platform systems complexes. There are ship-based, road mobile-based, aircraft-based, submarine-based and silo-based weapon complexes.

Ship-Based Weapon Complex

Consisting of a launcher system and a fire control system, this was first installed in an R-class destroyer, namely INS *Rajput*. Indian Navy is currently operating five such vessels: INS *Rajput*, INS *Ranvir*, INS *Ranvijay*, INS *Rana* and INS *Ranjit*. These five vessels form the backbone of the striking power of the Indian Navy.

The important process is integrating the missile complex electronically, physically and mechanically with the vessel. We will see the individual systems one by one.

Fire Control System (FCS)

As the name indicates, it controls the firing of the missile and it is in this system that the launch control switch is situated. The prime function is route planning, wherein it is decided how the missile should fly and reach the target. To reach a target, the missile can be made to fly directly in a straight line or in a curved path. Apart from this, the FCS maintains direct contact with the missile and reports about the health of the missile.

Contemporary ships have various sensors as the eyes and ears of the vessel, and have missiles as the main firepower. All the inputs from the sensors and weapon status systems are pooled into one station referred to as combat direction centre (CDC). The captain can conduct the battle from the CDC. (In the past, the captain had to be at the tallest point of the vessel to give his commands. His cabin there was known as the 'bridge'.)

The brain of the CDC is the combat management system (CMS). The CMS is connected with the FCS of many weapon systems present in the vessel. All sensors like radar and sonar are connected with the CMS, from which the FCS takes its inputs.

Man–machine interface (MMI) is the buzzword in contemporary weapon systems. Easier the operation, greater is the efficiency. When we were designing the FCS of the BRAHMOS, we kept the MMI as a top priority. The FCS has a number of graphical user interface (GUI) systems for effective MMI. The FCS carries out self-checks, link checks with external systems, and missile health check. It receives target data from the CMS. It also facilitates the operator by providing the combat and route planning for the missile when the target coordinates are provided. In a nutshell, the FCS is an interface between the missile and the operator.

Universal Vertical Launcher Module (UVLM)

When the target is in front of the vessel, there is no operational problem and the missile can be fired directly towards the target. But a war does not unfold as per prediction. If an enemy vessel is trailing our vessel to attack, the missile may have to be launched and programmed to take a circular course towards the enemy. However, the greater speed of the missile limits some sharp turns. So we developed a launcher that could launch the missile vertically from the ship. It was the universal vertical launcher module (UVLM). Its design has since been patented.

The launcher got its name because it can be directly used in any kind of vessel including submarines, destroyers and frigates. We wanted one launcher as a system to be fitted on to any type of surface vessel or submarine.

The greatest advantage of the system is that it can store more missiles than the inclined launchers. Not just that, more than one UVLM can be installed in one vessel. So, if two UVLMs are used, a single vessel may comprise 16 missiles – in effect, 16 different targets can be attacked in quick succession.

Technological Hurdles

The general principle in shipbuilding is that around 20 per cent of the space is reserved for installing systems that will be developed in the future. In general, a ship can serve a navy for around 40 years, and during these 40 years the techniques of war and weapon technology can undergo any number of changes.

The challenge for us was integrating BRAHMOS with an old vessel; it was not that easy. The INS *Rajput* was commissioned in the 1980s and the missile was integrated in 2003. The electronics systems belonged to the 1970s era

Next, it was time for INS *Ranvir*'s maintenance and repair. As a follow-up, the Indian Navy asked us to install the BRAHMOS missile in the vertical launch configuration. Foreseeing such a stage, we were ready with our UVLM by this time.

We had to alter the vessel by cutting some of the portions in the upper deck and removing them to accommodate the UVLM. A tedious process of degutting and integration was carried out in the docks of Vizag, a coastal city in the eastern seaboard. Finally, a flight trial was conducted successfully.

After the R-class ships, it was the turn of vessels like P-15A and P-15B, the new Kolkata-class destroyers, and the Talwar-class stealth frigates. The vessels P-15A and P-15B were equipped with 16 missiles, and the Talwar-class frigates had 8 missiles.

At this point, it will be prudent to explain the potency of the ship-based weapon complex. In the given figure you can see a sketch of a naval attack scenario in salvo mode. An early-warning helicopter belonging to the squadron is patrolling well ahead of the squadron of vessels. This helicopter with its high-power radar detects the presence of enemy vessels and relays the directional coordinates of the targets to the squadron. After proper authorization, the vessels will fire BRAHMOS missiles according to the requirement.

In the figure you can also see some decoy targets. Decoy targets are created by chaff clouds. Chaffs are nothing but a thin foil of aluminium-like metals that can reflect the radar signals. Generally, radar reflects signal, indicating that there is possibility of a target. So chaff clouds can deceive the radar by posing itself as target. The BRAHMOS has adequate intelligence to discriminate the actual target from the false one and can accurately home in on the target.

A group of some small vessels with an early-warning helicopter would be a deadly combination for the enemy to defeat. If ocean surveillance satellites are operated to scan the area continuously, they can also send target locations to the vessels directly. Such a surveillance platform will be the order of future wars.

Road-Mobile Weapon Complex

There are two variants of the land-based weapon complex: one is for land attack and the other is for coastal defence. These variants are almost similar in nature. The prime constituents of the land-based weapon complex are a mobile command post (MCP) and mobile autonomous launchers (MAL). One MCP commands four MALs and are collectively known as one battery – a basic unit. The MCP in turn gets its command from a command, communication and control (C3) centre. The battery also includes a workshop vehicle for conducting repairs, a mobile replenishment vehicle (MRV) for loading the MAL with missiles, and light combat support vehicles (LCSVs).

The MAL and the MCP are communication-intensive systems having a robust and redundant wireless voice and data connectivity. The communication is thoroughly encrypted. Some techniques are followed to prevent any jamming attempt by the enemy.

Mobile Command Post (MCP)

The future wars are going to be based on network-centric warfare (NCW) and the road-mobile weapon complex is a starter for that. MCP is one of the primary nodes in the NCW hierarchy.

The MCP takes commands from the higher echelons regarding the targets designated for that particular battery. The MCP designates the targets for each MAL, gives the target coordinates, fixes the number of missiles to be launched, and the time of launch. The MCP monitors the status of all MALs. In case any one of the MALs has developed a glitch, another MAL from the battery is assigned that task. Depending upon the terrain and situation, the MCPs are delegated the tasks that are sent turn-wise as commands to individual MALs.

Similarly, in a coastal battery, the MALs are given a set of targets to destroy and also instructed whether to launch in salvo mode or not. As I have said earlier, war is dynamic in nature and targets and target priorities can change at any time. Any change in target assignments is also catered for. The data of all the events in the MALs before and after launch are recorded, based on which the after action report (AAR) is generated.

Another important function is the analysis of terrain – this is done from the cartographic data to select a suitable deployment site for the MALs. The area through which the missile has to fly is also analyzed. For example, the target from an MAL may be at a short flight distance but if there is a hill then the missile has to circumvent the hill. Such issues are addressed by the MCP. As a true command centre, the MCP has a clear tactical picture of its area of responsibility (AOR), which shows the MAL deployments and the threat scenario.

Mobile Autonomous Launcher (MAL)

The MAL is a missile launcher system capable of carrying and launching three missiles. The word 'autonomous' is relevant. We wanted to make the MAL a self-contained vehicle – one that would not depend on other numerous vehicles for various requirements. MAL has a launching station, generator systems and many more systems. Though there are some support vehicles in the battery, the MAL is a highly independent system. Also, there could be a technical hiccup with the MCP or in an unfortunate moment the MCP may get destroyed by enemy action. After all, 'anything can happen in a war'. The MALs have been designed in such a fashion that in the event of loss of an MCP, any one of the MALs can take over its role.

The FCS is the predominant unit of the MAL—similar to the FCS in a ship-based weapon complex. In the MAL the missiles are kept in a horizontal position during storage and transportation. They are articulated to a vertical position at the time of launching.

The MAL is capable of launching the missiles in single or salvo mode. As you know, one missile battery contains four MALs, which make a total of 12 missiles, and each can be fired in rapid succession. So a missile battery has firepower packed to bring down 12 targets within minutes.

Aircraft-Based Weapon Complex

Work is underway to integrate the missile with the Su-30 MKI aircraft of the Indian Air Force. The Su-30 aircraft has a phenomenal range. When armed with the BRAHMOS, they will fetch a name as a deadly pair.

The aircraft modifications are being carried out at Hindustan Aeronautics Limited (HAL).

Simultaneously, we have undertaken the design of the airborne launcher. The launcher is as important as the aircraft modification. The aircraft will undergo aerodynamic validation tests for the launcher by carrying it under its belly.

Fitment of the missile in the Su-30 MKI aircraft

BRAHMOS – A is the name for the air-launched version of the missile. The missile has undergone some modifications for weight reduction. You may remember that the propulsion system is composed of a solid propellant booster and a ramjet sustainer. The booster is supposed to accelerate the missile to a supersonic speed from zero speed. Being carried by a fighter aircraft at high altitude means that the missile is exposed to sufficiently fast air flow. Whilst the booster does the same job, for this version it need not be heavy since its extra weight will consume extra fuel from the aircraft, thereby reducing its endurance. So we are reducing the size of the booster for accelerating the missile to a sufficient speed.

At the launch command from the pilot, the missile is dropped horizontally. The missile undergoes a freefall for a certain height and then it stabilizes itself, which is when the booster is fired. During the free fall and the firing of the booster, the missile has to be in a stable orientation. For adding stability, we have added small tail fins to the missile.

Peripheral Control Device

The aircraft has its own computer – the flight computer – as the centrepiece of its avionics. The flight computer gets inputs from all sensors and communicates with the pilot through displays. From the movement of various pilot controls (throttle stick, etc.), it understands the intentions of the pilot regarding the flight path. Accordingly, it actuates various aerodynamic features. Actually, it is only the flight computer that flies the aircraft, but it flies according to the pilot's instructions, which he gives through his flight controls. The missile has its own OBC that directs the missile to the target. This computer needs the location of the target, which is supplied by a peripheral control device (PCD). The PCD communicates with the missile's OBC and the aircraft's avionics.

The pilot in a typical anti-shipping mission will turn the aircraft's radar in the sea-search mode and when he finds the target, he selects it. The coordinates of the target are fed into the PCD. The PCD feeds the target coordinates into the missile's OBC. When the pilot squeezes the launch trigger, the missile gets released from the launcher and starts freefalling. The missile stabilizes itself to fire the booster. Then the routine programs in the missile's OBC are executed. The sketch here depicts the BRAHMOS-A missile being used in the anti-ship role.

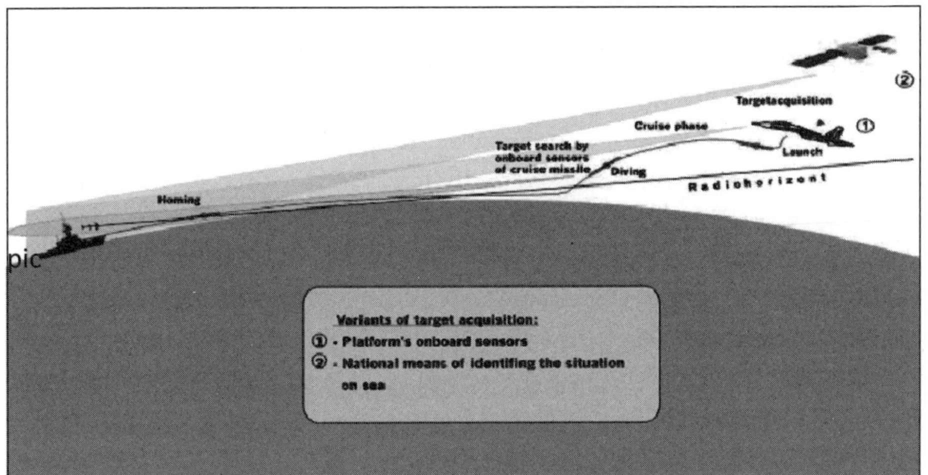

Typical engagement of an enemy vessel using the air-launched version

SUBMARINE-BASED WEAPON COMPLEX

The submarine is a complex and stealthy machine. Present-day nuclear submarines can travel at tremendous speeds and remain submerged for longer durations. When armed with missiles they become a deadly hidden predator lurking to take its prey. Today, every nation is trying to get a nuclear submarine and install their ICBMs in them. Doing this gives the assurance that the adversary will not launch his nuclear missiles so as to prevent retaliation from the opponent.

At the same time, the submarine is also a dangerous place to work at – the many operational hazards may take an enormous toll on the psychological health of its crew. Accidents may lead the submarine to sink and may also prevent the crew from escaping the sinking submarine.

Currently, the Indian Navy is operating the German HDW-class submarines as well as the Russian Kilo-class submarines; the French Scorpene submarines are under construction. The BRAHMOS missile is fully ready for integration with a new class of submarines called P75 (I).

This will be in the vertical launch configuration, making it one of the most powerful weapon platforms in the world.

Since the BRAHMOS is a universal missile, no alteration is needed. The nose cap will protect the missile by not lettingwater enter the canister. The presence of the canister will save the missile from the seawater.

However, there are challenges in integrating the missile with the submarine. The pressure underwater increases tremendously. Anything that has to survive underwater must be a hard nut. For us, the challenge is to degut the hull of an existing submarine to integrate the BRAHMOS. A slight miscalculation or even a small bit of disproportionate work may lead to a catastrophe, leading to loss of the submarine and the crew.

Very complicated modifications have to be made on the hull of the vessel with clinical precision. An enormous amount of simulation studies have to be carried out as well.

The underwater variant of the BRAHMOS missile has been flight-tested and is ready for induction. When the submarine gets the target coordinates (through a satellite or transmitted from a submarine command centre), it launches BRAHMOS and moves away from that area. The BRAHMOS missile can also be launched to hit land targets.

SILO-BASED WEAPON COMPLEX

Silos are underground launchers that are constructed with hardened concrete tubes closed with a hatch. Missiles are kept inside these silos. Since these facilities are underground, they are difficult to destroy and can even withstand a nuclear attack. So, silos are strategic assets from which a nation can return a missile strike.

When the requirement arises, the hatches are opened and the missiles are launched. During the Cold War, many of the nuclear-tipped ICBM systems of both sides were located inside silos. They provided deterrence by assuring a mutual destruction second only to submarines with nuclear missiles.

BRAHMOS is capable of being launched from silos. A fuelled and combat-ready missile can be deployed in a silo. If required, the missile can be fired at short notice. When the missile is placed inside the silo, the scheduled check-ups can be performed without taking it out of the launcher.

These silos can be constructed and a weapon complex installed near strong points along the coastline. A silo-based weapon complex will consist of (a) silo-based launchers, (b) a control centre from where the launch will be controlled, and (c) an underground or over-the-ground command post reinforced with heavy concrete layer. This command post will be connected to the higher echelons through various communication links.

A schematic sketch of a coastal defence scenario is given here. A similar weapon complex can be established for attacking land targets also. The enemy will also know that our missiles can finish the war even before it begins. That way, a non-nuclear deterrent can be established with these systems.

Into the Future: NCW Capabilities

Warfare has been evolving through various stages and at each stage it is centred on some attribute. The very primitive form of warfare was human-centric. Even up to some four hundred years before, warfare was human-centric. It was the number of the soldiers and their valour that determined the outcome of a battle. The army that had a huge manpower was considered strong. During Napoleon's era, warfare turned towards 'mobility and marching'. An army that was capable of manoeuvre was considered strong; a manoeuvrable army could quickly encircle or separate the enemy. In the 1900s it was platform-centric warfare, where superior weapon platforms like aircraft, warships and tanks, their firepower and numbers determined the outcome of a battle. Now we are in the age of transition to network-centric warfare (NCW). The future wars are going to be network-centric wars.

What is Network-Centric Warfare?

According to Sun Tsui,

> "If you know the enemy and know yourself, you need not fear the result of a hundred battles; if you know yourself but not the enemy, for every victory gained you will also suffer a defeat; if you know neither the enemy nor yourself, you will succumb in every battle."

The concept of the NCW is somewhat similar. If we know where the enemy is and what he is doing, and also know where our force is, then winning the battle is almost a given. How can we know about the position of the enemy? And after knowing that, what can we do?

There is the buzzword C4ISR, which stands for command, control, communications, computer, intelligence, surveillance and reconnaissance. When these entities are closely interlinked, they result in network-centric capability.

In a typical war, the offensive capabilities of the enemy and his defensive line must be assessed first. For that, the enemy has to be continuously monitored by employing surveillance assets. A typical example is an imaging satellite. Apart from that, a closer-level reconnaissance must be carried out by employing assets like aircraft with imagers. By analyzing these data, intelligence is gathered and that is the knowledge on the enemy.

After the assessment, proper planning is required to attack the enemy at his weak points and to strengthen our defences at our weak points. The plan has to be executed in close coordination at predetermined times; so the execution has to be commanded and controlled properly from the command centres. The decision-making command centre will be far from the frontlines. So, flow of command to the frontlines from the command centre and flow of reports back from the frontlines to the command centre is necessary. A delayed report or command can change the outcome of the entire battle.

After attacking the enemy, there should be battle damage assessment (BDA). This is to confirm the destruction of the target; if the target is not destroyed, another wave of attack is carried out.

In a nutshell, every single unit is connected to the high command through the immediate command. The high command can access each and every individual unit in realtime. Such a robust communication link will enable improved information sharing. The information sharing will give a complete picture of the battlefield, which in military parlance is known as 'situational awareness'. This situational awareness will lead to better command and control and hence mission effectiveness.

Imagine a scenario where an early-warning aircraft detects a huge enemy aircraft formation that has to be intercepted. Some friendly aircraft are also on the air, returning from another mission. These aircraft cannot be directed against the incoming enemy formation. Why? Because the status of the friendly aircraft may vary; some may be out of weapons or fuel and some may be damaged. The command must first know the status of the forces. When the command knows all the minutiae about the friendly aircraft, it can choose the aircraft that are fit to fight and can be sent to intercept the enemy. How does the command have all the information? Here comes the role of communication links.

Communication Networks

Each layer in the theatre is networked with each other – submerged submarines, surface vessels, infantry and tank columns, aircraft and satellites, etc. This may look simple but is very difficult to realize since each and every military unit has to be connected. If there are 1,000 combat aircraft in the air and 1,000 infantry platoons operating on the ground, just imagine the extent of communication involved. The most complicated issue is that every class of military unit operates in a different frequency band in the communication spectra. And even in a single band, the requirement will be huge chunks of voice and data communications, and that too in realtime. Not surprisingly, any one side's superiority in network capabilities will decide the course of war. Like Sun-Tsui said of the NCW, 'the weapon is going to be information and flow of information.' The targets will be the enemy's network, and every network will have their own choke points, their vulnerabilities. Hitting at these points will damage or degrade the enemy's network to reduce his combat capabilities.

> If a target is situated in a coastal city, a decision will be made on how the attack has to be carried out. It may be carried out by a ship-based weapon complex, a land-based weapon complex, or an aircraft-based weapon complex. If attacking from the land, the instructions are passed on to the individual MALs operating at a point from where an easy strike can be achieved through the MCPs. The MAL will decide the route plan and then the missile will be fired. The reports will be sent from the MALs to the higher echelons through various encrypted communication channels.

The BRAHMOS in NCW

The BRAHMOS missile system was developed to be a node in the network-centric capability of

Indian forces. The land-based weapon complexes, both the land attack and the coastal defence variants, have been developed as NCW-capable. The present sea-based weapon complex will automatically become an NCW element when the carrier vessel becomes compatible. Similarly, the submarine-based and the aircraft-based complexes will be NCW-capable when the corresponding platform changes so.

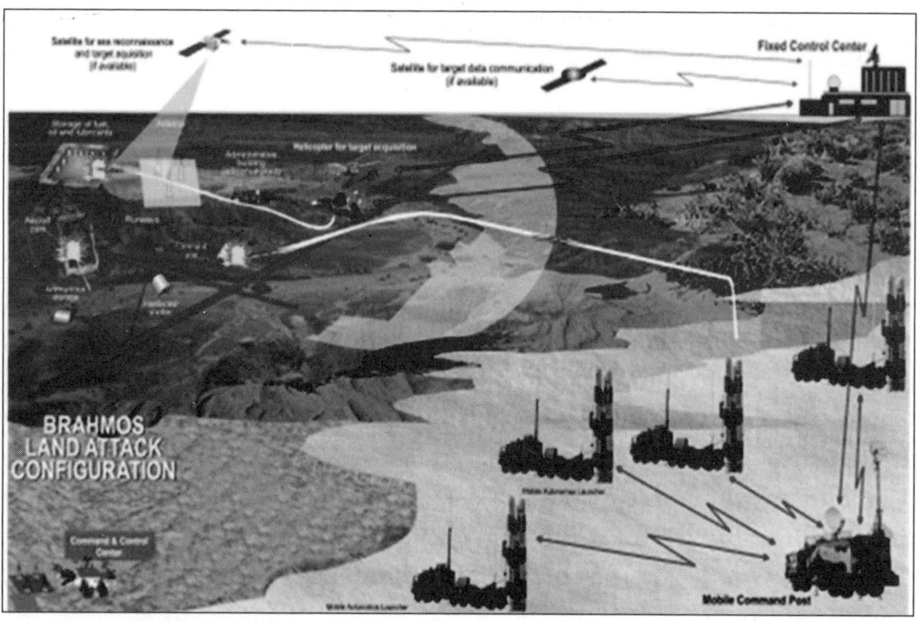

Schematic sketch of NCW with BRAHMOS inland-attack role

When the entire structure attains network-centric capability, the BRAHMOS system will easily fit in the new networks that are built. The figure shows a schematic sketch of BRAHMOS in land-attack missions.

PART 5

Courage in Rough Seas

"There are no secrets to success. It is the result of hard work, perfection, learning from failure, loyalty and persistence."

– Colin Powell

There were difficulties for us and we had to put in all our efforts to overcome these. For the uninitiated, the nerve-racking moments we faced during the flight trials would be beyond the realms of imagination. So, let me take you back in time.

11

The Flight Trials

Flight trial is the dynamic evaluation of various subsystems for their ability to perform in an integrated manner to achieve the set mission objectives. In a way, it is the culmination of development efforts on ground.

A missile has major subsystems like propulsion, structures, control, guidance, electronics, software and telemetry, along with power supply, connectors, junction boxes, relays, logic circuits, processors, many kilometres of cables and so on. Each unit has to go through qualification tests to meet the required environmental conditions specified in military standards. This rigorous testing and assessment of reliability ensures efficient functioning of the unit. Once such tests are complete and certified by the inspection agency, the units are assembled into subsystems, which again get qualified for integrated performance on ground under different levels of testing. Then come the interfaces between the subsystems as required in the checkout complex. During checkout, electrical performances of individual subsystems and interfaces are cleared with specific conditions of approval outlined in the procedure.

In order to verify the integrated performance to meet the specific missions, the missile is 'flown' on ground through hardware-in-loop simulation (HILS). Here, the flight of the missile is simulated by giving an external input to the sensor. To explain, let us consider the pressure gauge that monitors the pressure build-up in the missile. Pressure gauge generates more electricity when the pressure increases. The guidance system checks the increase in electricity and understands that the pressure is increasing. During HILS, the pressure gauge is replaced and a signal is injected manually, quite similar to connecting a small battery for electrical signal. Now, to simulate the increase in pressure, one more battery is connected. This test validates that a particular subsystem is working according to the design. Yet, all this may not be sufficient. Several failure modes are also simulated to study the effect. The mission algorithm also gets proved in HILS. Then we are ready for the flight test of the missile.

The said subsystem has to work in the actual flight. For each flight trial, a set of test parameters are fixed and then tested. Now, how do we know that a subsystem is working while it is flying with the missile? For this we need an electronic system that can transmit the missile performance to the ground. This is the telemetry system. On-board telemetry is needed to record the performance of the subsystems and in order to enable ground units to receive the data and large computers to process the data. This gives real-time analysis of whatever is happening to the missile. During the flight trial, we can see a real-time trajectory plotted in front of us in the control centre, thus communicating the actual performance of the missile.

All these flight trials are observed by a group of personnel from the armed forces. Once they are satisfied, they give a set of simulated combat scenario. These are the user-defined flight trials and are carried out according to the combat requirement of the user. Once the objectives are met – that is, the target is hit under the simulated combat scenario – the system becomes ready for deployment. In addition, an elaborate training of the army personnel is carried out to ensure the readiness of the system for actual deployment. For further assurance, field trials are carried out by the trained crew from ship for the navy and from desert or a mountain region for the army.

After induction, the users conduct the flight trials themselves. These are termed as user flight trials. There, the user is the one who operates the systems and the scientists who developed the system supervises the trial. The results of such trials give confidence to the user for war preparedness. The deployment process starts.

Let me now describe the action scenario during the countdown in a flight trial.

What is Countdown?

Most of you would be aware that a counting sequence is done in the reverse order during flight trials. Why it is done? And what is done during that time? Here I will describe a typical countdown process for aerospace missions, whether it is of ISRO or DRDO or NASA. For representation, I will use the term 'missile'.

The missile is a highly complex system with thousands of subsystems that may work individually or sequentially or as groups. A subsystem may be required to work only for one second. For example, there may be a valve whose functionality is to open and close. Simple in words, isn't it? The real complexity is its timing. That valve has to open at the exact second. Its opening a second before or later may even lead to a catastrophe.

Then comes the human factor. It is a mission and therefore several agencies are involved. The place from where the missile launch is to be performed is called missile test range. This range needs to be ready with all safety clearances to give the go-ahead for the launch. A flight NOTAM (notice to air and marine movements) is issued to avoid traffic during the launch. All the tracking radars, telemetry stations, computer network and safety operations are networked and put in operation in the range. The naval ships are deployed near the target points with telemetry stations on the ships as well as helicopters to acquire the data on the target hit. Also, at the launch point, a number of telemetry and tracking systems including radar and electro-optical systems, data processing centres and mission control centre are all activated in a network form. The integrated coordination and the proclamation of the countdown sequence are carried out at the mission control centre. For each mission, its overall control is governed by the mission director who integrates the missile, the ground complex, range systems, meteorological data, range safety, the down-range stations, the communication network, the processing centre and emergency operations.

Once a flight trial is planned, the first parameter to be checked is the viability of the meteorological conditions required for the missile launch. Next, the time is fixed for launching the missile. Then we calculate back and set the clock for countdown. This time period is called the preparation time for the missile to be ready for launch. For example, our PSLV requires a preparation period of 60 hours. There are systems that require even 96 hours of preparation time. Each and every subsystem involved in the mission, whether in the missile or on the ground, is thoroughly checked and made ready for the launch.

If the missile is a liquid-fuelled rocket engine, like Prithvi, then preparation time is required for fuelling. It is to be noted that fuel, being corrosive in nature, is not filled beforehand. Once it is fuelled, then the missile has to be launched and cannot be stored beyond a certain time. Fuelling is a process that has to be carefully carried out to avoid any catastrophic explosion, as the fuel and oxidizer used are hypergolic (instantaneous explosion on contact). Since the BRAHMOS has storable aviation-grade fuel for its ramjet engine and solid propellant booster, the countdown time does not include fuelling.

There are many such activities that fall within the preparation time. All these activities are managed through coordination of time and space. The reverse countdown synchronizes all these actions.

While describing the count-down, I thought of an interesting episode to share with the readers.

My son Dr. Bhagavath Kumar is a Surgeon, who after his specialization M.Ch. in Plastic Surgery at Stanley Medical College, Chennai went to USA for fellowship in Micro and Hand Surgery. My grandson, Sivathanu Kumar who was only five years old at that time, telephoned me from USA and asked "why in India, they taught me to count from 1,2,3, … 10, whereas in USA, they start with 0,1,2,3, ... 10." I said since, '0' has no value, we start counting from 1. He caught me by saying, "Grandpa, you showed me the video of launch of a missile. When they get ready for launch, they say 10,9,8, ...1, 0. When they say 'Zero', then only the missile leaves. So '0' is important." Indian schools should also realize the value of '0'. He bowled me out straight. I felt that Indians who found out Zero, should count up from 0, 1...

Generally, the exact instant of the launch is called as T0 (T Zero) regardless of the time in the clock. If there is 30 minutes to launch, then that time is referred to as T0 minus 30 (T0-30) minutes. After the missile is launched, the time is counted in normal sequence. So, two minutes after the launch is called T0+2 minutes. During the countdown, all the actions are executed in a coordinated sequential manner. Each group confirms that they have executed their share of task.

The mission director announces the start of the countdown. As the countdown progresses, every system and operation gets confirmed for readiness. The mission director authorizes launch in auto mode. During the last few minutes, typically T0-6 minutes, the automatic check-out system takes full control. The check-out system gives the signals for various operations for full readiness of the missile and checks the parameters for correctness. The authorized fire control officer presses the fire button at the destined time. The missile gets activated and takes off. Then we start counting up and announce the parameters being displayed on the monitor till it hits the target. The flight trial team can instantaneously tell that the flight trial is successful. The mission director announces the fulfilment of the mission objectives and thanks all the participants. Within the next two hours, the post-flight analysis team presents quick-look results to confirm the performance.

I have participated in flight trials from land and sea from the days of SLV-3 to Agni to BRAHMOS. It is full of tension as the launch campaign team never want their hard work to fail. The flight test can be a success or a failure, as there are more than a hundred thousand components that have to work as expected. Discrepancy in performance of a single component may result in mission failure, even though every subsystem is checked thoroughly and prepared with enough care. Once the mission succeeds, it is a great sight to see the faces of all the personnel who were involved in the flight trial operations. To be sure, flight trials trigger emotions on unimaginable scales.

Flight Trial Locations

Generally, missile flight trials are conducted at the Integrated Test Range (ITR) at Chandipur-on-Sea near Balasore, Odisha. It is a beautiful place for tourists. The Bay of Bengal recedes four kilometres during low tides and the waves will be in full blast during high tides. This happens twice in a day and is an interesting sight to watch. During low tide one can walk on the sea with bare feet and collect shells (seaweeds). The British had located this site for trying out firing of shells (ammunitions) from artillery guns. This establishment is today called Proof and Experimental Establishment (PXE) and has completed more than one hundred years.

At the Integrated Test Range, whenever we launched Agni we needed to evacuate nearly 3,500 residents from the nearby villages in order to have the required safety clearance. While the villagers obliged without any problem, there were considerable difficulties. We needed a safer range. That was the time we were also looking for a land target for the Prithvi flights, as we had to prove the accuracy of impact to the Army. The Wheeler Island off Damra (in Odisha) could give a 70 km range from ITR. The Prithvi launch took place successfully, impacting close to the target on the Wheeler Island, Dr Kalam decided to use the Wheeler Island as the launch pad for Agni and its future bigger missions in order to avoid the evacuation of people during launch. He met Mr Biju Patnaik, the then chief minister of the state, and asked for the site. Mr Patnaik immediately agreed and said, "Dr Kalam, you must launch the ICBM from Wheeler Island and make our country strong." Today, Agni-V launched from the Wheeler Islands fulfilled the dream of Biju Patnaik and Dr Kalam.

The test range has a wide array of instrumentations like tracking radars in multiple bands, electro-optical tracking systems (a kind of camera) in visible and Infra-Red lights, Fixed and mobile telemetry stations, tele command stations, range safety, meteorological stations, real time data acquisition and process computers, camera stations, etc. This facility became state-of-the-art facility for testing missiles and aerial vehicles. We utilized this location very well and all our developmental flight trials were conducted from here. Similar facilities are available in the Wheeler Islands and its nearby shore.

The other location is situated in Pokhran, Rajasthan. It is called Pokhran Field Firing Range (PFFR). This area is extensively used by the Army and the Air Force to practise firing of their equipment and weapons for their armament evaluation. We used this range for testing our warheads used for Prithvi. The other range is ship. Navy carries out their trials at Sea, with ship as the launch pad.

1. THOUGH THE MISSILE FELL

As we prepared for the first launch at the ITR, we started loading the missile in the static vertical launcher exclusively erected for the BRAHMOS system. For loading the missile inside the vertical launcher, it was necessary to lift the missile to double its length and slide it inside. The missile was being lifted through a crane with a special lifting device holding the nose cap. When the missile reached 15 metres above the ground level, the holding device inadvertently yielded and broke. The live missile fell down, back on the corsette – the transport trolley, making a loud noise. It was a pathetic scene and the operating personnel ran away for safety. A live missile is terribly dangerous even if it is without any warhead. Everybody held their breath. Slowly some of them gathered courage to approach the missile for observing any abnormality. We got the information and swiftly acted to isolate the live missile for detailed examination by experts. Our Russians friends suggested that we destroy the missile by following a procedure. That was what they did in their country.

For the flight test we had prepared two missiles: the main and the standby. With the main missile in an accident, we did not have time to lose and loaded the standby missile after taking corrective measures for the loading fixture. The launch was successful.

Next, we studied the fallen missile and made an elaborate plan to check each subsystem carefully and analyze the results. We were satisfied with the health of the missile and decided to go ahead with a flight trial instead of destroying it. Conventional wisdom said a dropped missile could not be flight-tested as there was the possibility of an internal failure. But the Indian team took this as a challenge and after careful review of risks decided to carry out the launch. After great convincing and showing them the results for every subsystem, the Russian side also agreed to the launch. The launch authorization board (LAB) cleared the launch. The launch (FT 02) was hundred per cent successful and our scientists were even more jubilant than they were after the first successful flight. Such was the robustness of the BRAHMOS. What was equally important was the decision making process and not afraid of failures. It paid off immensely.

2. Launch Operation From MAL

No machine is complete unless the man using the machine is competent. As a military machine is used in adverse and frequently changing dynamic situations, the man operating it should be highly competent. The man behind the machine plays a significant role in exploiting its full capabilities. Yet, human interface with the war machine is the last in the chain of proving a system. This is because the safety of the system has to be proved by successive trials.

So, the missile was to be test-fired from the ITR to validate its operation from a mobile launch complex with an advanced guidance system and manoeuvring trajectory meant for the Indian Army. Several activities were at full throttle in preparation of the launch from a mobile autonomous launcher (MAL). The Army had posted a specialist team to take over the missile group and they were spearheaded by Col. Bishnu Ram.

I still remember the indomitable spirit of our colonel as he volunteered to launch the missile from the MAL itself. Normally, till the time the system design is frozen and development is complete, such an adventure is not advisable. In this case, the safety concerns were huge as the missile was to fly over his head. The missile was loaded with hundreds of kilograms of propellant. Any mishap would result in a catastrophe and failures were a part and parcel of flight trials. Even developed nations like the USA and the USSR had faced failures in flight trials and lost their astronauts and cosmonauts. You may be aware that Yuri Gagarin was the first man to reach space. He was a test pilot and he died when he was test-flying an aircraft. So accidents can happen at any time.

Our Colonel here said, “Sir, my organization has placed me here with some purpose. This system belongs to us and I have grown with the system. I must launch the missile from the MAL as per the ultimate configuration of design.” I was overwhelmed by the courage and faith of the officer on the system. He showed the finest traditions of the army, ‘displaying selfless devotion and leading from the front.’

Eventually, the confidence of the colonel convinced us to go ahead with his plan. I knew the worth of the system, but the thought of the one-in-a-million possibility of failure was at the back of my mind.

Meanwhile, the head of the FCS division Mr VSN Moorthy volunteered to join the colonel in firing the missile from the MAL. Here, I have to laud his guts and grit. Normally a scientist thinks twice before taking a risk. Although our Russian friends advised us to opt for a remote launch, by then we had decided to go ahead with the launch with our men inside the MAL. I spent sleepless nights pondering the issue of MAL launch with our men. I was worried because it was the first such experience for our missile team. If any mishap occurs, it would be a disaster and the end of BRAHMOS induction in Army. But the sheer grit and courage shown by our men was negating the risk and helped us to overcome the worries. We mounted a big contingency plan at the launch pad to face the worst.

The destined time came. After saying our prayers, we wished both men good luck. They stepped inside the MAL at the scheduled time. I remembered the Apollo 11 mission in July 1969, when Neil Armstrong, Michael Collins and Edwin Aldrin walked inside the Lunar Module LM 5. In the same style, our friends walked inside the MAL. Both officers were calm and showed no sign of hesitation. The launch pad was evacuated and we settled in the blockhouse in front of the consoles. The CCTV cameras were inside the FCS cabin of the MAL to monitor the crew conditions. The crew with their smiling faces comforted us and the countdown was initiated. The atmosphere inside the blockhouse was tense. Our lips went dry as the final few seconds came. Till that time there was no glitch and everybody sat with their fingers clenched and crossed. An emergency vehicle was waiting outside the blockhouse for me to rush to the launch pad, in case of an emergency. The teams were alert to face any eventuality. The countdown reached the final ten counts. My heart started beating fast.

10...9...8...7...6...5...4...3...2...1...Zero!

The command was given. An ear-shattering thunder rose. If any of you live near the airport, youmust have complained about the noise of the flying aircraft. The level of noise that a missile launch creates is exponentially higher and is hard to endure. Amidst that thunder, the missile came out of the canister like a shining sword coming out of the scabbard. It rose high, rolled, pitched and started its supersonic journey right above the fire team. The blockhouse broke into applause and tears of joy. Yes, the launch was a success! The capability of the MAL was proved beyond anybody's doubts. I rushed to the launch pad to look at the courageous fire team, who emerged victorious without a single scratch. Their victory smile still shines in my eyes and will remain forever. I recalled to them the words of Neil Armstrong, "That's one small step for man, one giant leap for mankind." The fire team was thrilled to be the first-ever crew to fire a supersonic cruise missile for the land force. When inducted, I told them, the Indian Army would be the first land force in the world to have a land-attack supersonic cruise missile.

Col. Bishnu Ram commanded the first ever BRAHMOS regiment for the Army and Mr VSN Moorthy, a DRDO scientist, is now project director of BrahMos. These men have certainly made their proud place in the history of BrahMos for firing a supersonic missile over their own head. Now, it is a routine practice since all our Army-version missiles are launched from the MAL. In recent times, a young courageous lady scientist ANS Prasanthi conducted the launch sitting in the MAL cabin along with the Army crew. The same MAL will be used by Indian Air Force and next by Indian Navy for coastal defence.

3. A Cyclonic Trial

One of the flight trials was conducted at the ITR in the month of June, the south-west monsoon period. We intended to launch the missile to test some of the crucial parameters including advanced software and guidance. Unknown to us, Mother Nature wanted more from the missile. She wanted the missile to prove its all-weather capability.

All the requirements were met and launch procedures were carried out systematically. Then, almost out of nowhere, a severe tropical cyclone had formed in quick succession in the Bay of Bengal and was supposed to cross somewhere around the eastern coast. When we reached the ITR, the sea was rough and roaring to its full might, a scary sight for us. It is known that the wind and sea conditions during a cyclone are not at all favourable for launch of missile. In our case the wind was roaring with a speed of around 150 km per hour, as reported by the ITR's meteorological set-up.

During any flight trial, we follow a set of procedures to clear the flight tests based on what is called flight readiness review (FRR). We were in the middle of the FRR meeting on the cyclone day and debated whether to conduct or abort the mission due to the met warning. Some were in favour of the launch and some others were against it. There were strong winds and chances of heavy rain in the next morning when the launch was scheduled. We decided to wait for a minimum level of favourable weather on the next day; if there was no improvement, we were to pack our bags to Hyderabad because the meteorologists reported a storm approaching.

That night, we could barely sleep due to the apprehensions about the next day's flight trial. It could prove to be an ultimate test for all the men and the machine. So many thoughts were battling in the mind. The missile had to prove itself with tall mission objective and which would be a proof for us. The Rain started to pour as if a chorus to the whistle of the gusting winds. I was not able to sleep due to the anxiety and opened the windows of my room from where I was able to see the sea. Indeed it was a fearsome sight to see the roaring sea. Like the waves of the sea, my thoughts were also oscillating and I discovered that my colleagues were also spending sleepless nights.

Why I am stressing over this is due to the fact that war is not a cricket match that can be called off due to rain or whose result can be decided with the Duckworth–Lewis method. War may erupt at anytime and weather is an important feature that militaries take advantage of. Think of a similar situation on sea when the ships are subjected to heavy roll and pitch in different conditions. Still the men in uniform on the ship have to fight the war. They have to launch the missiles to attack the enemy ships. Basically, all the resources, men or machine, must be in fighting fitness even in adverse conditions. So, while one cannot escape proving the efficacy of the system in adverse conditions, it may not be advisable to take risks during development tests to prove new objectives.

Next day, early morning, I went out to have a look at the sea waves and the fury of the wind. I met many of my team members at the seashore. I went to the new guesthouse where the Russian specialists were staying. The door could not be opened as the wind from the opposite side was blowing in full throttle through the door that was kept open by them. All our Russian colleagues were in the balcony looking at the sea. After I called them, a gentleman tried to open the door but it would not open. He again asked us to push the door from outside. The door still did not open. So the people inside the room joined hands to open the door. The culprit was the door facing the balcony. When that door was closed, the other door could be opened. When I went inside, I saw this strange group and one of them exclaimed, "Nature treats everybody equally!" Ripples of laughter started shaking the room due to this timely comment.

It was raining like anything; imagine how the cyclonic rain together with gale winds would feel in a coastal area. Amid this, there was a sudden clearance in the weather though it was far from favourable. Yet, it was the only concession that nature seemed to offer for our launch. We did all the preparations in quick succession. Vice Adm. Arun Prakash, the then vice chief of Indian Navy, joined us to witness the launch. As the user arrived, we saw a sudden patch of light as the clouds gave way. The sun appeared. We acted fast and took the decision of going ahead with the launch.

The countdown reached its most crucial last phase. In that short period of time, we felt as if we are going to receive the question paper of some practical examination—students of science and engineering disciplines can understand the problem very well! Even for experienced professionals, the last phase of countdown is a test for patience and endurance. Then, as the wind started increasing its speed,a warning came that a cyclone might be crossing through that area very soon. The mission was held back from launch as the range director did not consider the situation conducive for the launch.

A decision had to be taken –whether to conduct the trial in high wind speed or to call off the mission. I asked my team to go ahead with the launch and not to worry about the wind speed, which had just reached its extreme limit. The whole team including the then project director Mr Venugopalan was prepared to take the risk. The hold was lifted. The countdown started.

On the count of zero, the missile took off. It rose up into the sky and then carried out its journey in what was a textbook performance. The take-off picture clearly showed how severe the wind was. Even to move the exhaust of the booster to one direction was a herculean task. We realized that the missile was so robust in its control system design and structure that it could withstand such severe weather conditions. In particular, the inertial navigation system of DRDO technology performed beautifully. It was a great experience of decision making with risk. I had the feeling that God was a partner to the BrahMos project.

The famous British poet Alexander Pope once said,

> "Nature, and Nature's Laws lay hid in Night.
> God said, 'Let Newton Be!' and all was Light."

Like his words, the performance of the missile even in adverse weather tore through the screen of pessimism.

The astonishing performance of BRAHMOS was understood by Adm. Arun Prakash and other user friends who witnessed the launch. This boosted up the user confidence tremendously which resulted in a quick letter of intent for BRAHMOS in multiple ships for Navy, signed by Vice Adm. Arun Prakash, the then Vice Chief of Naval Staff.

4. The Andaman Launch

An Island, Please!

We had to prove the land-attack capabilities of our missile when launched from a ship to a land mass having a target. This would enable the Navy to use the missile for coastal targets. Therefore, we decided to conduct a flight trial in the Andaman Islands, as it was not possible for us to locate land target in the mainland of India. Lt Col. Anil Misra, another hero, and I planned to carry out an aerial reconnaissance of the 572 islands of Andaman and Nicobar to locate our island for positioning a target. We had the help of the Navy and the Combined Command of Andaman & Nicobar (A&N). Many believed it would not be possible to get environmental clearance from the Prime Minister's Committee to carry out a missile launch on a land target at Andaman and Nicobar Islands.

The reason was the presence of rare species of flora and fauna in most of the uninhabited islands as well as islands occupied by the tribal natives. Still, we decided to first conduct the survey and choose the appropriate island to position the target for the BRAHMOS missile to be launched from a ship sailing in the Andaman Sea.

It was a wonderful experience to see all the beautiful islands and the Andaman Sea from a naval aircraft. Though, it was not a joy ride but a mission, still we were unable to resist admiring the beauty of the Islands. We flew over the volcanic Barren Island, which we first thought of as installation place for the target. But it was not suitable for our mission. Going south of Port Blair, one of the Islands of Nicobar got our attention – it was Meroe Island. Adjacent to the Meroe Island there were two more islands, Trak and Treis. After the complete survey, Col. Misra and I met the forest range officers, the chief secretary and the lieutenantgovernor to put across our proposal for Meroe, Trak and Treis islands to be allotted to BrahMos for its missions. We convinced them that the missile was accurate and that the target would be positioned in the large sandy area, leaving a small portion of rock and a few coconut trees. I assured them that not even a single coconut tree would be affected in the process. We wanted to ensure that the target location was decided based on the ground reconnaissance on these islands.

Lt. Governor got excited with the suggestion and boldness to ask for the islands to be allotted. He asked me to come to his residence that evening for a tea, with a laptop containing presentations. I went to his residence that evening. The Lt. Governor received me at the living room and I saw many snacks items including my favourite items – Madras Mixture & Murukku. Lt. Governor said that first you show the BRAHMOS launch video again. I want my wife also to see. I showed the launch video. His wife exclaimed that what a wonderful missile. India is safe. She told the Governor – you must fulfil his aim to carry out the flight tests at A&N Islands. Finally we got a preliminary green signal from the administration.

Adventure to the Island

On the ground, the idea of undertaking a foot reconnaissance was quite adventurous. The team comprised of Colonel Uniyal, Lt Colonel Anil

Misra, AD Rane and Joint Managing Director Alexander Maksichev. You may have heard that sportsmen, especially cricketers, are highly superstitious. But missile scientists are more superstitious than anybody else. Our team looked for an auspicious time and sailed in the survey vessel INS *Sagardhwani*.

Unfortunately, the sea was very rough and it started pouring heavily. Everybody was courageous on the face of it, but the sea conditions were sending shivers in their spines. They rang me up from the ship and informed the conditions to seek my decision to call off the journey to the island. I asked them to proceed further without fear as everything would be alright, because I had a firm belief that God was also our partner. As they approached the island, two of the members got into a 25 HP engine fitted on a small Gemini boat that was normally used by the naval divers. They were joined by an executive officer and two expert divers from the Navy.

With a roaring engine, the Gemini started its journey from the ship towards the island. It was still pouring and misty. From the ship, the boat looked like a fading dot appearing and disappearing between blue waves. When they were about 10 metres short of the beach, high waves toppled the raft throwing all the five members on the beach on their heads. Two members reached the shore with great difficulty but with scratches all over the body, as the shore was rocky. Immediately the Navy team dashed back into the sea to get hold of the Gemini, which was being snatched away by the waves. They were thrown away by a huge wave. Somehow the Gemini was pushed into the sea to fetch the second set of members.

Now, on the ship, the second group of landing party was preparing to board the Gemini and they jumped into the unstable boat. Hundred metres before the beach, the diver requested all on-board to help him in holding the Gemini to avoid a similar incident as in the first trip. This group was unaware of the hazards of beaching the Gemini. They jumped on to the beach by holding the Gemini from opposite ends. But in a fraction of a second the Gemini was on top of them; only the inner instinct of survival made it possible for them to immediately come out of the dangerous situation. The Gemini was somehow pulled to the beach. The fact was that one of them did not know swimming and he had to somehow beat his hands to move to the shore. After regaining their orientation and getting over the initial shock of the head-banging landing, the team started their tasks.

They made an effort to go over the entire island, which was ultimately not possible either due to the rocky face of high banks or due to dense forestation. Even walking on the beach with drenched clothes was tiring as the foot sank by four to five inches in the sand. Astonishingly, all the electronic systems that accidentally got soaked with seawater and sand worked well! Unluckily, though, the drinking water that the crew was carrying was lost. With bruises all over and the body drenched with salty seawater, these men went about their work. They located an ideal site over a large sandy portion for erecting the target. The location was decided taking into account that the missile hitting the target would not affect the ecology of the Andaman and Nicobar Islands.

Getting the Islands

After a detailed survey of the islands, we made our plans for a possible launch site from the sea and a place to position the target. We got all the clearances from the Government in record time. The administration had changed by then. Lt Gen. (Retd) Bhopinder Singh had taken charge as Lt Governor of the Andaman and Nicobar Islands. He was earlier the military secretary to Dr Kalam when he was President. We knew each other very well. So everything went on top speed. The Lt. Governor, Chief Secretary and the Forest Officers all were supported the mission unanimously. We assured them that there won't be any damage to the flora and fauna of the islands because of BRAHMOS, as we were sure about the accuracy of BRAHMOS in hitting the target. Everyone was thrilled and wondered if such a mission was possible. Thanks to Col. Misra, our hero who toiled to get these islands for BrahMos. Then it was necessary to get clearances from MoD and Government for conduct of the launch.

Alas, the Tsunami Struck

On 26 December 2004, a tsunami struck the Indian Ocean as a result of an earthquake with an estimated energy released on the earth's surface at 1.1×10^{17} joules, which is equivalent to over 1,500 times that of the

Hiroshima atomic bomb. The tsunami hit the islands with a magnitude of 9.0, with the epicentre off the west coast of Sumatra. The violent movement of sections of the Earth's crusts – called tectonic plates – displaced an enormous amount of water, sending powerful shock waves in every direction. The massive tsunami devastated the flora and fauna of the Nicobar region. The saline water had completely damaged the greenery of the entire region and some of the islands got submerged in water. The northern islands in Andaman and Nicobar lifted up by 1.5 metres and the southern islands went down by the same height.

It was a disaster that held back our mission. We came to know from the administration that an Indonesian ship got stuck close to the beach of Meroe Island due to the tsunami. Col. Misra and I again undertook an aerial survey to inspect the fate of our islands and to decide over the launch. I saw the watermark of the islands in the northern portion which lifted up and the lighthouse at Indira Point down in the sea, and also the heavy damage to all the trees of the islands with seawater logging inside. We went to Car Nicobar and met our brave Airmen. They forgot all the agonies and started talking about BRAHMOS induction in Air Force. The central portion of Meroe Island was severely damaged and there was sea erosion in Trak and Treis. We decided to shift our target point to the seashore of Trak Island. We had to desert Meroe after seeing its condition and also to avoid the foreign ship that was stuck there. The administration told us that the abandoned ship could become a target for BRAHMOS after one year if it was not recovered by the owner. All preparations started for the launch from INS *Rajput* in the Andaman Sea towards the target that had to be erected at Trak.

Is that an Enemy?

A five-member team consisting of Col. Misra (BrahMos), Rane (DRDL), Dhir (TBRL), NS Srinivas (RCI) and Satyanarayana (RCI) had to construct a target on the island, make necessary alignments of the target taking into account the trajectory of the incoming missile, and place high-speed cameras at suitable locations to capture the target destruction. A stand had to be constructed with metal rods. It was decided to land the team on the island through a helicopter. For dropping and supporting our team, the Indian Air Force came forward to help and they deployed one of their helicopters based in Car Nicobar. The helicopter was hovering over the island. When the team was about to get down from the helicopter, they saw some mysterious tracks similar to that of a truck. The team asked the helicopter crew about the tracks. The pilot of the helicopter turned his head towards the team and wished them luck with a mysterious smile playing on the corner of his lips. The helicopter dropped the team members one by one.

The team remained a bit apprehensive about the tracks. Luckily, the mystery of those tracks was unveiled by the first evening itself. It was discovered that the tracks were neither made by a truck nor had some strange creature visited the island – they were the footprints of sea turtles.

Intense Labour

With our team on the ground, we were onboard INS *Rajput* and were systematically preparing ourselves for the launch. The team was dropped on the island with all materials required for completing the target construction. No information was available regarding the rise and fall of tides. Still, they ventured into that unknown island. We were unaware of the amount of work that had to be carried out.

The team made a temporary shelter with tents. All of a sudden, heavy winds started to blow during the dark and it was later accompanied by rain. The intensity was such that it blew away the shelter. It kept raining for the next 24 hours. How did the team survive? They wrapped the tent material around them and sat on the sand with the lantern as the only ray of hope until next morning. The members passed the time by sharing their experiences.

They also had the none-too-friendly company of crabs. A large number of crabs attacked the edibles, cigarettes and anything they left over the ground. There was also a chance of being attacked by the crabs while they slept. So they collected dry coconut leaves around them and lit a fire to keep away the crabs. Turn by turn, each one of them kept awake to let the others have some rest.

After around 24 hours, the rain slowly ceased. The team started taking various measurements to construct the target, which took one full day. As there were some rocky barriers, the process of aligning the target got delayed. Finally, the place was adjusted and the construction started.

Here, I have to mention the support that was extended by the Combined Command of the Andamans. The command deployed one helicopter exclusively for this flight trial for ferrying between the island and the base. If I ask our team members about the best breakfast they had in their entire life, without a second thought they would mention the one they had on Trak Island. One crew member said, "After being soaked in rain for more than 24 hours, the alooparantha and the hot tea brought and dropped by the helicopter crew gave a new life to us."

The erection of the target structure was in progress. The target was divided into a lower section and an upper section. The lower section was a small pillar-like structure upon which the upper section had to be placed. The placing of one section over another had to be done by a helicopter. Could the structure stand still over sand? For that, they used pegs to secure the stand structure.

Now, the upper section of the target had to arrive in the helicopter. The team stood underneath the chopper to place the upper section on the tower. Have you ever noticed the gestures of people standing underneath a landing helicopter on a beach? The experience may be described thus in the words of a team member: "It felt like thousands of pins pricking simultaneously all over the body." Finally, both the sections were placed as designated. But the task was far from complete. The upper section had got placed over the tower in an angle that was not as per the plan. This meant that the upper section had to be turned for best fit, which was a herculean task in itself. Military personnel are trained to think out of the box for achieving crucial tasks when conventional ideas do not work. Col. Misra and Rane found the solution by improvising a turn buckle. They erected an extra peg on the ground and tied it with the iron cables attached to the structure through a turn buckle. Then using that turn buckle, they slowly turned the base structure to achieve the required angle.

I went to Trak Island in a helicopter and requested the pilot to drop me on the island to meet the team. R. Adm. Nair, the Deputy Chief of the

Combined Command who accompanied me refused to do so keeping in mind the safety aspects. He, knowing my adventurous mind, asked his men to tie up tightly with the seat belt. I asked the helicopter pilot to fly as low as possible close to the target. The helicopter made second round. I could see the target erected and I was satisfied. After all these actions, the team returned to INS *Rajput* after five days of hectic work on the island. They were tired and sick with full of blisters. As the missile was launched from INS *Rajput*, it flew all the way following the exact trajectory and penetrated the target. It was a perfect hit as confirmed by the helicopter crew. Our team got down on the island and collected the high-speed video cameras. The videos confirmed the precise hit on the target. We had proved one more version of the missile – sea to land. What a great achievement and satisfaction to the BrahMos team who put their whole-hearted efforts to locate the island, get the ownership of the island for conducting the launch, construction of the target in odd conditions and physical exertion, carrying out the launch at the Andaman Sea far from our operating shores. It was a great effort, yet the mission got accomplished with perfection. There is no equivalent experience of this sort except that we have read about adventures of Sindbad.

When I met the members of the target-erection team at Port Blair after the successful mission, my eyesight got blurred with tears. Those men had blisters all over the body, sunken eyes, and unshaven faces stuck with sand, but their eyes glittered. I have seen this light in the young scientists hardened by determination, working tirelessly in the labs and missile integration buildings, unmindful of time–space boundaries. I have seen this light in the eyes of people who burst into tears after seeing through the missile meeting its mission objectives. Once I visited the frontiers, I saw the same light in the eyes of our soldiers who fought with the enemy disregarding the bad terrain, weather conditions, and other personal emotions. It is this light of determination, courage and dedication that keeps the nation on the track of development. What a great Nation we belong to and the men of action when there is need! Hats off to my friends! They are the heroes of BrahMos.

5. Launch from INS Rajput - Clenched Fists

It was Navy's foresight to possess such a powerful weapon onboard their warships. Upon seeing the first flight trial, V.Adm. John DeSilva, the then FOC-in-C of Eastern Naval Command thought of finding an opportunity to get a ship for fitment of BRAHMOS. Fortunately, INS Rajput was on re-fitment. He advised Adm Sushil Kumar, the then Chief of Naval Staff to give this opportunity to BrahMos. When Admiral asked me over telephone, I immediately accepted and gave an accelerated schedule to match the refit time and install BRAHMOS. It was a great boon for us.

Integrating the missile with a vessel means that the missile should be connected electronically, physically and mechanically, and it takes huge amount of time. Electronically, the missile can be integrated by first installing the Fire Control System (FCS). Then the FCS is integrated with the shipboard electronic consoles. Similarly, the launcher gets integrated with the vessel. Our design team interacted closely with the Russian specialists who originally designed the R-Class ships to get the structural and load details and worked out the details of removing the existing launchers, reinforcement required and the new launchers to be fitted. Preliminary project report was prepared and reviewed with the design review committee involving Indian and Russian Specialists, members from Larsen & Toubro (L&T) and Naval Dockyard, and officers from Eastern Naval Command. A comprehensive approach was worked out for fabrication and fitment of the structure, launcher and also the electrical interface requirements for the FCS. The work progressed at the Naval Dockyard and L&T. All the tasks were carried out as per schedule within the re-fitment time.

Then it was a time for a flight trial to validate the performance of the missile and ship complex specifically made for BRAHMOS. In that trial the missile had to be launched while the ship was moving. The whole mission was reviewed thoroughly by the appointed Flight Readiness Review (FRR) team. A number of issues came up like the adequacy of the software in the FCS, the trajectory of the missile at take-off when the ship is pitching and rolling amidst extreme sea conditions, the possibility of the nose cap falling on the deck, the effect of the full blast of the booster on the deck at take-off, the type of sound which the crew had to handle, safety of the people, limits on the speed of the ship and so on. It was the first time, a missile of this size being launched by the Navy and the concerns were well understood. Risk is involved everywhere, but we were not afraid of the risks. A careful intelligent analysis is necessary to overcome any risk. With this determination, we cleared the launch. The launch was a great success. Now, Navy got a big boon that a long range supersonic anti-ship cruise missile was installed on-board the flag ship of INS Rajput - A historical moment for India.

Perfect hole in the target ship

The Indian Navy decided to fire BRAHMOS from INS *Rajput* for various flight profiles. So, as a next step the missile's targeting capability had to be validated. For every flight test we need a target. Generally, the procedure is to use decommissioned vessels as targets. Since they are actual ships, they replicate the target parameters accurately for any missile. So, navies generally reserve the decommissioned vessels for using them as targets in future.

For this mission, the Indian Navy allocated the decommissioned vesselex-INS *Androth* as a target. Being a decommissioned vessel, the engine, weapons and all other useful sections had been stripped off the vessel, and it had to be towed to the designated place for the trial. But the vessel was in such a bad condition that after reaching the designated place water started pouring inside. The flight trial became a question mark.

Fortunately, Commodore Chinnaverriya at BrahMos who had formerly been the captain of that very same vessel was with the team that towed the target ship. Generally, the captains of ships consider their vessels as their close companions. So, our man said, "I am not going to leave my companion to sink." He asked for volunteers. Men from the Navy stepped forward and a small team was assembled. The team went to the vessel in a boat, fighting the rough waves in the darkness. They worked all night to pump out the water. The vessel was afloat by daybreak and was staged at the designated place early in the morning. The target was declared ready.

Mr Venugopalan, Mr Kieslev and I reviewed the readiness and cleared the launch. The missile was launched in the morning on the dot. It took off beautifully with a roaring sound and pierced the target. A helicopter was sent to investigate the target's status. Commander SM Shiva Kumar, who was onboard the helicopter, was continuously updating me on whatever he could see. He said, "Target is located but it looks normal." As the helicopter approached the vessel, he reported a 'hole in the target ship'. The helicopter was taken around the other side of the target ship, after which he reported a 'big hole in the target'. That meant the missile had pierced through the target ship one metre above the water level, exactly hitting the middle of the hull. This was a bull's-eye hit. The trial was a great success and the Navy celebrated with a grand party at sea onboard INS *Rajput*.

6. Combat Launch: One Shot, One Kill

Having seen the successful flight trials with full user participation, a request came from Admiral Arun Prakash, who had then taken over as the chief of naval staff, to conduct a combat flight trial during their annual naval exercise. Normally, trials do not include testing with warhead. Assuring us of giving production orders and that no more trials would be conducted, Admiral Prakash demanded successful destruction of the target by BRAHMOS. I accepted the demand though it was a deviation from our plan. Our Russian friends said that this test must be conducted by the Navy on a missile to be declared as delivered. The Navy accepted the condition.

We quickly mobilized ourselves to conduct a test with live warhead on combat mode, off the Goa coast. INS *Rajput* was loaded with a missile and ex-INS *Sindhudurg* was chosen as the target ship. On 15 April 2005, I was onboard INS *Virat* along with Admiral Arun Prakash, Vice Admiral Sureesh Mehta, the then DCNS and other officers from the Navy. Our team with Venugopalan were onboard INS *Rajput*. We carried out the launch with a precise hit on the target, which split into two parts and sunk. All happened in no time. After the launch, we boarded a helicopter and went to see the condition of the target. When we reached there, the vessel had sunk completely. Only traces of the vessel's debris were found. We saw a boat nearby from which naval divers were waving their hands.

The naval divers had recorded the video of the missile hitting the target with a big bang, the target ship got split into two and sunk in waters. Later, they said the event happened so fast that the missile came and hit the vessel and it sank within minutes. The disturbance caused by the sinking of the vessel made it difficult for the divers to maintain the stability of their boat. Nevertheless, the videos displayed the enormous kinetic energy and the power of the missile. There was no match for the BRAHMOS. Admiral Arun Prakash kept his word and placed production orders to fit the BRAHMOS on multiple ships. He also authorized funds to design and develop the universal vertical launcher module for fitment in future ships. Indeed, it was a great partnership with the Indian Navy.

7. Desert Launch – Converting Anti-Ship into Land-Attack Missile

The BRAHMOS was originally designed to perform as an anti-ship missile with a radar seeker. In order to bring a new version for the Army, it had to be used as a land-to-land missile. In other words, the missile had to be launched from a mobile launcher equipped with a command-and-control system. The typical targets are ammunition dumps, missile bases, missile or ammunition factories, railway yards, airports, communication centres, critical bridges, and so on. A suitable seeker is required for homing in on these types of land targets. Generally, the option is to go for terrain mapping and a GPS-guided system. While we had started developing a scene correlation and area navigation (SCAN) seeker, to quickly work around a solution for the Army we had to adopt innovative methods that nobody had attempted ever.

Testing the Seeker

Generally, a seeker fitted over an aircraft mimics the missile trajectory (but not the speed). The output of the seeker is analyzed and based on that one concludes how well a target is detected, which trajectory it followed, what has been the angle, etc. An arrangement was made to conduct this analysis on a suitably modified Russian Tupolev-134 short-range transport aircraft. We thought of flying the aircraft specially fitted with the missile's seeker over various real targets to study their signatures in order to establish the adequacy of the seeker in land-attack mode. Our team reviewed the provisions of the telemetry systems and were happy with all the arrangements made to monitor the recording of the seeker. Our scientists were waiting for the Russian team to carry out the experiments.

That aircraft came with a string attached. It was conveyed that Indians were not permitted to fly in that aircraft as the aircraft belonged to another Russian agency, over which our partner had no control. We strongly objected to it. We contended that since it was a joint venture the Indian scientists had equal responsibility and right to conduct the experiment over our land. We asked the Russian agency to take back their aircraft as we were not in a mood to carry out any test over our land without Indians. The team accompanying the aircraft understood the stubborn stand of the Indian side and contacted their authorities. Because of our stand, they relented and we could utilize the aircraft. We guided the aircraft to fly over a variety of targets, thereby evaluating the performance of the seeker. We got excellent results and cleared the seeker for integration with the missile.

Flight Trial in the Desert

We conducted two consecutive successful trials for proving the land-attack version of the BRAHMOS. These trials are carried out at the Pokhran Field Firing Range (PFFR). Both the flights were witnessed by General JJ Singh, the then chief of army staff. Incidentally, the second trial conducted on 31 May 2006 became a summer trial. The Rajasthan deserts are known for their heat, and in summers the temperature easily exceeds 52°C. The conditions were such that the work had to be started very early in the morning and stopped by 10 AM. Only after 5 PM could the work resume. Here I must mention the willpower of our Russian partners. When we declared the launch, they wanted to participate even though the temperature did not suit them at all. In their country -20°C is a normal ambient temperature. The spirit showed by them was tremendous.

Building a Target

The missile had to be launched outside the PFFR, fly over two villages travelling on the desert, and hit a concrete wall specifically erected for this purpose at the designated target point. Constructing a wall in the hot Rajasthan desert was the most difficult part since the wall could not stand without a foundation, which could only be constructed by digging the sand. A concrete wall was constructed which would lean over a supporting pillar like a structure analogous to the photograph stand.

Target Hit

General JJ Singh reviewed the preparedness for the launch. He went through the mobile command post, the mobile autonomous launcher loaded with the missile, its standby, and the command centre. The countdown begun and, as usual, at T0 the missile took off beautifully, vertically up, turned towards the direction of the target, and quickly disappeared from our sight. The General and I quickly rushed to a helicopter to see the effect on the target. We found that the missile had finished its job long back. We built a helipad near the target for the General. From the helipad, we went by a four-wheel drive on the desert and looked at the target. With a glowing smile, the General congratulated me and said that the induction process must go on the fast track for the artillery division of the Army.

Nick of Time

When we celebrate success, we must remember how our young team members went through the difficult experience. Two of our engineers in their mid-twenties were present in a telemetry vehicle five to six kilometres behind the target. The cables of high-speed cameras located near the target to capture the hitting sequence were connected to the telemetry vehicles. The countdown was already initiated. It was just 90 minutes to T0. Suddenly the telemetry vehicle lost its signals. The two young engineers went in a vehicle to inspect the cable. They connected the cable that had snapped and were returning when the vehicle got stuck in the sand somewhere near the target. Unfortunately, their cellular phones were not reachable and by this time the countdown had reached 45 minutes to zero.

There was every possibility of the vehicle producing radar signatures that would be a source of clutter for the missile. The two young men were not ready to take any chance and needed to have the countdown halted. So they started running in the desert towards the telemetry vehicle by following the tracks of the vehicle. Those who have walked in the sand dunes of a desert under the hot sun can understand how tough it would have been. They ran with their feet burying in the sand and reached the telemetry vehicle and asked an army officer to communicate the problem in the wireless radio. Colonel Misra, who was associated with our development activities, rushed to his wireless radio to contact the launch point for holding the countdown. He was planning to hold the launch for some time so that he could send a vehicle to recover the stuck vehicle. Unfortunately, he was unable to establish contact and now the time left was just seven minutes to launch. He rushed to the spot in his vehicle and commanded the driver to turn back the recovery vehicle. From that point they could see the target, and after moving some 500 metres away from the target, they heard a sonic boom and banging noise simultaneously. The missile had penetrated the target, travelled further, and made its impact on the ground.

We were waiting at the launch point and could not establish communication with the lost telemetry vehicle. We had the information from other vehicles that the target was hit. Finally, the radio crackled and the Colonel informed us directly.

In private he told me that the two engineers were rushed to the nearby military medical facility just to have a medical check-up. I also rushed there along with the senior scientists. When the engineers saw me, their first question was, "Sir, is it a success?" I was amazed to see the commitment of the young scientists irrespective of their difficulties. I nodded my head in affirmation and blessed them. The grit and dedication of these boys moved me a lot. This reinforced my thoughts that a stronger new generation is getting ready to see the uplift of the nation.

8. Taste of Failure and Regrouping

We had successfully inducted the first regiment from 2007. The Army now wanted a next version of the BRAHMOS which would discriminate a particular target from among a group of targets. This needed surgical precision to locate and hit the target. More intelligence needed to be incorporated in the missile on-board computer and guidance system. We required a GPS receiver that would be compatible with multiple global navigation satellite systems as also a seeker tuned to home in on non-radio-contrast targets. This requirement was quite challenging and we started developing the system as BRAHMOS Block-II. The first launch of Block-II was scheduled for 20 January 2009. General Deepak Kapoor, the then chief of army staff, came to witness the launch.

In the Pokhran range, a group of five targets were constructed. They were not reflecting the radar energy (low signature) constructed with a thin sheet.

After short count down, the missile took off and headed towards the actual target. To our disappointment, the missile did not hit the target; it just passed above it. General Kapoor was dissatisfied with the performance and the Army informed the media that the flight trial was a failure. The media took it very seriously. In the history of BrahMos, this was the first incident of a missile not hitting the target. Moreover, it was a crucial time for our country since it was immediately after the 26/11 Mumbai attack. There was a huge outcry. On their part, the Army maintained an indifferent posture by saying that further induction would be carried out only after successful flight trials. I assured the Government, Army and the media that we would find a solution to the problem and within a month, next launch will take place.

Courage to Succeed

When I returned to New Delhi, I saw pale faces in the office. For the first time my team had tasted failure. The critical comments had left them extremely hurt. I called for a meeting in the evening and declared, "We will conduct a successful flight trial in a month after re-tuning the software."

I had already seen a major setback when I was at ISRO, during our first attempt to launch the SLV-3 on 10 August 1979. The same thing happened in the fourth launch of Prithvi in 1989 and the second launch of Agni in 1991. Failures are grounds for a lot of learning if we carry out the analysis carefully and draw the conclusions correctly. The second launch of SLV-3 on 18 July 1980 was a great success and further flights of Prithvi and Agni were consecutive successes. I narrated my experience with the Agni to my team.

The Agni Experience

Initially, Agni was a technology demonstrator to establish the re-entry technology with a two-stage propulsion system and the carbon composite re-entry structure with guidance and control. The first stage was a solid booster that was used in the first stage of SLV-3. We got the first stage from ISRO and went for a launch in 1989.

The Agni launch campaign was a special one, full of technical, managerial, social and political challenges. It was all set to make its first test flight in April 1989, after six years of painstaking efforts in developing various subsystems and conducting a large number of ground tests. The launch campaign commenced on 31 March 1989. A special launch complex was made operational in the Missile Test Range at Chandipur with many instruments for tracking and telemetry.

The launch countdown started on 20 April 1989. At T- 6 minutes, the countdown went into the automatic mode controlled by the checkout system. All the systems got actuated and checks were continuously carried out one by one to keep the missile ready for lift-off. At T-1 second the launch was aborted due to hold given by the computer as there was a problem in the umbilical pull-out. The hold was not lifted by the mission director in time, resulting in aborting of the mission. It would now require a detailed review of all the power packages before the authorization of launch.

There were many important visitors including the defence minister, the cabinet secretary, the defence secretary, and the three chiefs of staff. Before chaos could take over, Dr Kalam took control of the situation. A detailed analysis of the failure was carried out on the same day and the rectification started. The whole system got refurbished and a special effort was made to clean up the first-stage control system with the help of the

ISRO team. The system was made ready within 10 days and launch was attempted on 1 May 1989. Again, during the countdown at T - 3 seconds there was a failure in the first-stage control system. One of the injection valves gave way leading to leakage of the secondary injectant. The mission was aborted by the automatic checkout system. There was a crisis. The Government was very unhappy and put the Agni launch on hold. The newspapers of those days were full of cartoons depicting Agni as an interminably delayed ballistic missile (IDBM).

For us, the situation was grim. We did a quick failure analysis of the control system package and found out that the proportional injection valve cracked due to stress corrosion. Many components in the first-stage control system had to be redesigned and fabricated.

Hundreds of scientists and staff members of ISRO worked round the clock for 12 days and rectification action for the first-stage control system was completed in record time. The integrated system went through all acceptance tests and the system was cleared by a specialist committee.

When I reached DRDL and met Dr Kalam, he informed me that the Government had not yet cleared the launch. We had to persuade the concerned authorities in Delhi with complete information and assurance of a successful launch. We succeeded. Launch campaign started once again in the midst of continuous criticism from the press and other external pressures. The Indian Airlines and the Indian Railways facilitated the movements of hundreds of members for the launch campaign, even though there were no advance reservations. The Air Force extended continuous support by providing aircraft and helicopters. The Navy with their ship-borne stations and the Army through their medical facilities also helped. At Chandipur-on-Sea, about 12,000 people had to be evacuated for safety reasons, within an area of about 3.5 km radius from the launch pad. A combined effort was made with the local administration to move people, give them proper shelter and food, and make necessary arrangements for their safety on the launch day.

Finally the day came. On 22 May 1989, the countdown was smooth and Agni took off majestically and completed its mission successfully. The criticisms and abuses were forgotten and the whole country rejoiced in the mission's success. It was a great day for India as we entered the elite club of countries having long-range missiles. Interestingly, on 24 May 1989, a cyclone hit the range and heavy rain started pouring in the following days.

Having narrated my Agni experience, I told my dejected team members, "The factor between us and success is just a matter of time; the challenge is to compress the time." The entire team geared up and everybody regardless of their work profile was ready to contribute.

We carried out a detailed analysis with all the concerned engineers and chalked out a programme along with the Russian specialists to validate the new software and to carry out necessary simulations. The corrective measures included more sensitivity to the seeker to track low-radar energy from the target with dynamic computations to give error details to the on-board computer and logic for correction with the INS. All these problems do not occur with a long-range mission, which is the real application. Here, in the desert, the range is very limited and the time of flight is short and the speed is supersonic. The software corrections were incorporated taking into account these factors and the whole mission was simulated for a number of times. This time we were quite sure that the target would be hit. Hence, we informed the Army that we were ready.

The Army was hesitant. There was new pressure to look at alternative imported systems. Disregarding all apprehensions, we proceeded with the desert launch with great confidence. The launch took place on 4 March 2009 and the missile hit the target. This time, the deputy chief of army staff had come to witness the trial.

Sujan Dutta and GS Mudur wrote about the success of the BrahMos in *The Telegraph* on 3 April, 2009.

Missile Man pierces army apathy
How a tenacious technocrat put the supersonic BrahMos back on track

New Delhi, April 3: India can stake claim to be among the first in the world to be ready with a supersonic land-attack cruise missile because of the tenacity of an unheralded Missile Man whose pet project was almost written off for aiming too high.

Sivathanu Pillai, a technocrat whose bald pate is not covered by berets, whose chest is bereft of medals and shoulders of epaulettes, dared the Indian Army by claiming he would arm its artillery divisions with a missile the world had not seen.

The Army said they wanted one more launch to establish the reliability of the missile. I smiled and immediately agreed. Multiple targets were created in the desert. The target chosen was the least signal-emitting thin sheet. This was a real challenge. On 29 March 2009, the flight trial was conducted in the presence of the director general of military operations. The missile discriminated the specific target among the group of targets, flew straight towards it, and hit precisely. We declared the Block II readiness to all. Soon thereafter, we got production order for two more regiments of the Army.

Failure is an inherent part of any high-technology development, particularly when trying to achieve new missions and stretching the potential of the weapon. Failures give better understanding of the system and contain lessons for the future.

There were many, many special experiences that the BrahMos team has gone through and shared. On all occasions during the last 15 years, the members displayed a high degree of integrity, commitment, courage and value. I was fortunate to have such a wonderful team with me. This was acknowledged by the great men who participated in the celebration that marked the completion of 15 years of BrahMos – as Aardhik Diwas (Partnership Day) – on 19 February 2013.

PART 6

All Hands on Deck

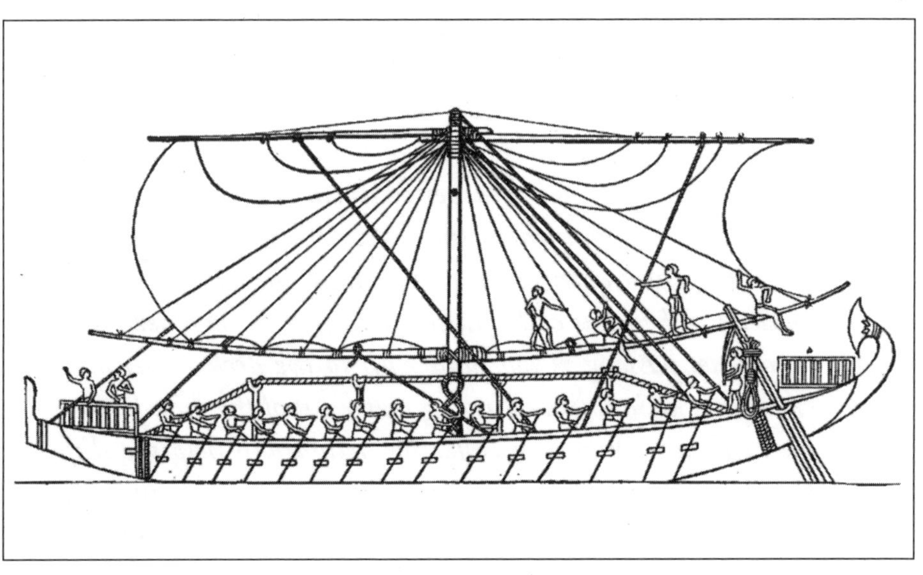

"Coming together is a beginning, keeping together is progress, and working together is success."

– **Henry Ford**

'All hands on deck' is a naval terminology used to tell all seamen to get to their stations or positions and prepare for action. It is also an expression one utters when everyone's help is needed, especially to do a lot of work in a short amount of time. During rough weather or during an emergency, the ship has to be manned to the fullest efficiency. For such a situation, the captain instructs to raise the call 'all hands on deck'. When this call is raised, all the crew members, and sometimes passengers too, will rush to the deck to perform emergency actions like pumping water out of the ship, furling the sails, etc. Only such collective action will help the ship to come out of the crisis. The entity BrahMos too was the result of collective effort and the joining of hands by disparate entities...

12

A Fusion of Great Minds

Anybody will agree that India and Russia are entirely different in their cultures, languages, weathers, and so on. In due course of the project, the enormity of those differences came home to us all too well. Both the sides put in genuine efforts to understand and work with each other. Only our mutual determination won the day.

Working Culture

Working culture involves adherence to time and quality of work. The Russian culture dictated that both these parameters be met but in the said time. For example, our Russian friends used to stick to office timings. They used to enter the office two minutes before the opening time and will nowhere be seen in the office two minutes after the closing time. In contrast, for us Indians the momentum seemed to pick up after the closing time of office. All the important issues used to be discussed after 6 PM. We would retire very late in the night and be back to the office on time. One afternoon, during the days of the IGMDP, a good friend came to meet me while I was in a review meeting. My assistant told him to come by 10 AM the next morning. But he insisted in meeting me on that day itself. My assistant told him that I might return late at night. My friend, who thought late meant somewhere around 8 PM, waited on the couch. After the meeting got over at 2 AM, I saw somebody was sleeping on a couch. He was none other than my old friend. He was in deep slumber.

For an Indian, quality work can be completed with marginal relaxation in time; for the Russians, quality work has to be completed within office time. In fact, many of our Russian friends used to say that a work not delivered at the right time was inferior in quality. Ultimately we learnt that important lesson and started to follow the same. To our customers, our products would be delivered well ahead of time – which was contrary to the Indian scenario.

Language

The biggest barrier was language. Russia is almost a single-race country with one language. On the other hand, India is a subcontinent made up of different peoples with different languages, dialects and accents. For us, the common connecting language was English. All the Russian documents, names of the systems and their sub-sections used to be in Ruski (Russian language). Our documentations were all in English, which the Russians were not able to understand. For us, interpreters became a necessity.

Initially, the funny thing was that the majority of the interpreters and translators were from an arts and Classics background. They had given up science at the high school itself. And what they had to translate was totally high-end technologies. So they were forced to learn the scientific jargons in both English and Ruski. Luckily, some of our scientists had studied in Russia. They came in very handy during the meetings. Many of our scientists were able to learn Ruski in course of time, and the Russians also learnt to speak English.

Bridging Standards and Specifications

Indian scientists were familiar with the western standards in every aspect of engineering, from design to documentation, and so on. The Soviet Union, which was once known as the iron curtain with everything shrouded in secrecy, followed their own set of standards and specifications. Thus, a bolt of Soviet origin would never fit in with a western country's nut, and vice versa. For us, then, there was bound to be a mismatch, in miniscule pieces as well as huge and complex systems. Wherever possible, the existent missile systems were matched with the Indian standards; under impossible conditions we simply accepted the Russian standards for smooth functioning. This proved to be a strategic move as it reduced the time considerably for working with the Russians; however, it came at a price – difficulty.

The electronic systems that had been developed in India were with Indian standards of protocols. This necessitated the development of new intermediate systems that could match both Russian and Indian protocols. These systems accepted Russian protocols and extracted data from them, and then sent out the data in Indian protocols.

Numbers were extensively used to denote projects, developed systems, sections and subsections. This was very quite different from the naming conventions followed in India. Initially the use of so many combinations of numbers used to confuse us a lot, but we gradually got accustomed to it. For instance, three Talwar-class frigates were being built by Yantar shipyard at Kaliningrad in Russia for the Indian Navy, and the BRAHMOS missiles had to be installed as the primary weapon system. This meant that the Indian design team had to work closely with the Russian designers so that the ship and the missile system were compatible.

Cuisine and the Climate

As we grow up, we develop a certain taste with respect to the food we eat. Other cuisines may be enjoyed but not on a daily basis. Indian cuisines are centred on spices. In contrast, Russians prefer their food without spices. When the Russians visited India, the food used to be too spicy for them, and when we went to their country, the food was tasteless. So, for both sides a tour to the partner nation used to result in stomach problems due to the difference in food preferences. Gradually, as the visits became more frequent, we established a Russian corner in the Delhi office cafeteria and an Indian corner at NPOM. Now we were sharing not just missile technology expertise but also the art of cookery. Russian ladies were specially trained to make Indian food at the NPOM kitchens.

The climatic conditions also posed severe problems to our scientists. When the preliminary design review was scheduled, it was winter season at its peak in Moscow. We were advised to buy some Russian winter clothing before setting off. When we wore those warm clothes, it felt as if our body weights had doubled. We joked that we had become astronauts, medieval knights, etc. Even then, we were shivering inside the armour-like clothing. Somebody informed that the temperature was a bit on the hotter side on that day. We were unable to control our smiles as the temperature was actually 25°C below zero. Exposed to such cold temperature, it felt as if there was no nose and no ears due to the numbness. We spent around three months over there and after returning back and shedding those special clothes, we felt weightless.

The Indian weather also troubled our Russian friends. One of our flighttrials was conducted in Pokhran during the last week of May. The ambient temperature was 52°C and the launch campaign was scheduled for 20 days. The Russians used to wrap themselves in cloth soaked in water. They had a hard time in the desert as well as at Chandipur-on-Sea due to the high humidity.

For all of us, the mission was bigger than anything else and we adjusted according to the situation.

13

MEN OF WISDOM

In both countries we had to interact and work with many top politicians, ministers, national leaders, service chiefs, senior scientists and bureaucrats. There were many nice experiences and these will stay etched in our memories.

THE FIRST FLIGHT TRIAL

The design of the missile was decided by the time the company became operational. Initially we did not have the facilities to integrate the missile in India. So all the necessary components from DRDO were sent to Russia and these were integrated with the remaining Russian components. The final missile was secretly brought by an Indian Air Force transport aircraft. Even the transport crew was clueless about the content of the container. At that time only the top brass of the three services, the top bureaucrats in defence ministry and DRDO knew about the project. A date was fixed for the trial; it was 12 June 2001. In Russia the date is celebrated as Russia day.

We were both confident and nervous. Mr Jaswant Singh (the then minister of defence as well as external affairs), the three service chiefs and the top brass from DRDO and NPOM had assembled at the Integrated Test Range (ITR), Odisha. The countdown began and everyone's attention was on the monitor in the blockhouse. At T0, the missile came out of the launcher. And a new era in missile warfare began.

JV so far was the top-secret project, but any flight trial conducted at ITR would come to limelight. Hence, it was necessary to get the permission of Government for the flight trial and also releasing the news on the results. The then prime minister Atal Bihari Vajpayee – the man of wisdom, who was in complete knowledge of the BrahMos project approved the announcement of the joint venture programme and release of the news about the flight test.. The whole world was stunned by the successful launch of supersonic cruise missile by India.

From that day itself, the company started to grow exponentially and every month there has been steady progress. Before the flight trial, nothing was sure like whether the defence services would buy the weapon and in case if they don't what would be the future of the project, etc. But within minutes the missile cleansed all those negative thoughts and injected confidence to the users, particularly to the Navy.

Inauguration of Corporate Office by Vladimir Putin

Almost a year after the first flight trial, we got land for our corporate office in the New Delhi Cantonment area. We decided to construct a guesthouse and a state-of-the-art corporate office on that land. We also hoped to have the office inaugurated by Mr Vladimir Vladimirovich Putin, the then president of the Russian Federation. In the year 2004, our office building was almost ready. We wanted the office to also hold a permanent exhibition of the history of the Indo–Russian relationship and the technological prowess of NPOM and DRDO, the shareholders.

As Mr Putin's visit came closer, we came across some unforeseen problems in the construction and found ourselves lagging behind schedule. The security agencies visited the buildings and the surrounding areas. The team consisted of some Russian protocol officials and after they surveyed the incomplete structures they started bawling. They conveyed to us that they could not include the inaugural function in the itinerary of the Russian president. Difficult though it was, finally we convinced them that by the time of the president's arrival everything would be in place. We had just about 10 days to the ceremony.

We had to apply concurrent engineering practices to carry out a variety of work in rapid phases. Masonry work and electrical and plumbing fittings were carried out simultaneously along with interior decoration. One night before the ceremony, all the tasks were complete for the security agencies to take control of the buildings.

The next day, Mr Putin came and said he was happy to associate himself with a world-class high-technology project resulting out of cooperation between India and Russia. During his speech he lauded the successful joint venture. He said that BrahMos "should be the model for all future joint ventures with foreign countries." Mr Putin stayed at the complex for more than the scheduled 20 minutes and showed great interest in knowing the details.

In 2005, when I went to Kremlin with the then President of India, H.E. Dr APJ Abdul Kalam, on an official visit, I had the opportunity to convey to President Putin that his recently issued decree made the JV difficult to function as every interaction with Russian industries had to go through Rosoboron export – the intermediary agency for Russia's exports/imports of defence-related and dual-use products, technologies and services. I requested for a waiver for BrahMos as otherwise there would be difficulties in procedure, leading to heavy delays. President Putin noted the point and soon a special decree of the president was issued maintaining the status quo between BrahMos and NPOM.

In another incident during MAKS 2011, Mr Vladimir Putin, the then Prime Minister came to witness the Hypersonic programme of consortium Institutes of Russia. While entering the Hall, he located me standing away, rushed towards me along with the accompanying officials, hugged me and got apprised of the latest status of the JV. This simply shows how a leader of his stature gives importance to India-Russia collaborative programme where success is delivered.

First Delivery of the Land Based System

Dr Kalam after becoming the president earned great fame as "The People's President." By the year 2007, our land attack version for the Army was ready and production process was progressing. We organised a ceremonial function on 21 June 2007 as a mark of the beginning of delivery of systems. It turned out to be a huge function attended by the Defence

Minister Mr AK Antony who declared that day marked a historic day for the Indian Army. Gen. JJ Singh who received the missile from the Supreme Commander of the Armed Forces expressed his happiness to posses the most potent missile for the Army. President Kalam declared that BrahMos has made India the first and has broken the Fifth Nation Syndrome.

Interesting Businesses

The First One

In the first flight trial the missile was launched vertically, and in the second it was launched in an inclined position. Immediately, the then chief of Indian Navy told us that we should test the missile from their ship. Anyone would expect the first business to be on credit. No! We requested money from the Navy to integrate the missile in their ship. The chief looked at me stunned but sanctioned the money with a smile. This was the first money dealing with our customer and it so became that we started the business with a debt.

The PM Came to Our Stall

In the military business sector, international military exhibitions play a vital role. These exhibitions are the launch pads for business campaigns for selling military hardware. BrahMos Aerospace is an aggressive marketer in such military expose and it becomes necessary to fetch export orders. In the beginning, we wanted to establish and familiarize the name of the product internationally. In 2001, we participated in Langkawi International Maritime and Aerospace exhibition (LIMA). Though we were just a minor in the eyes of many, our presence caused several raised eyebrows. For other exhibitors and military business tycoons, our presence was strange. They were accustomed to the Indian presence in the capacity of delegates and visitors.

Initially we were able to secure a remote corner in the exhibition hall due to our late registration. The then prime minister of Malaysia Dr Mahathir Mohamad, who was inaugurating the expo, came for a visit and with a curious look he entered our stall. There were only three of us; myself, the Indian ambassador for Malaysia, and Vice Admiral De Silva, the then vice chief of Indian Navy. It was a relatively small stall; we had a few posters on display and videos of flight trials being played on the laptop. After seeing the videos, Dr Mohamad was impressed and instructed the chiefs of the defence services to keep an eye on BRAHMOS as it could give an advantage with its accuracy and speed. In the meantime, other exhibitors became curious due to the amount of time spent by Dr Mohamad at our stall. Soon we were to be swarmed by various service personnel and other bureaucrats from the defence ministry of Malaysia.

Another interesting event was during "La Feria Internacional del Aire y delEspacio" or simply FIDAE. FIDAE is a defence expo conducted in Chile and an important event for the arms sellers. During this exhibition we were a well grown up company; a big team was representing BRAHMOS. Chile government enquired us about exporting the missile to them. Informally, officials revealed that Chile was going to buy the missile system from us. Later, Mr Pranab Mukerjee, the then Defence Minister, was on an official visit to Chile. He conveyed the Chilean Defence Minister about BRAHMOS and ALH. Later, we came to know that someone blocked that deal. Marketing is not so easy, even with the best product we have. We have to manage the under currents also, with honesty. That is the challenge. When I visited Pentagon later, its Naval Fleet Commander had all the praise for BRAHMOS and was not ready to leave my hand. He also expressed that the Indian Navy possessed tremendous power with BRAHMOS as its prime strike weapon. An Indian Vice Admiral, who was with me, acknowledged the statement made by that Naval Fleet Commander.

In another international expo, a delegation from one of our neighbouring countries visited our stall. A Major General – the leader politely asked whether we can explain about the BRAHMOS system. As it was an exhibition, we were obliged to display the normal presentation material to highlight the importance of BRAHMOS and its capabilities. He expressed his happiness on the frankness and wished good relation between the two countries. He however whispered to me whether India is prepared to sell BRAHMOS to his country. I could not resist my temptation to respond to his question. I told him "BRAHMOS is a free delivery item to his country".

14

Missile Industry Consortium

A major lacuna in indigenous defence production is the non-availability of quality products, produced in adequate numbers and realized in a predefined time. Moreover, the success of a product depends on its competitive value in the world scenario.

Product competitiveness is based on (a) product excellence (performance, quality, reliability); (b) cost-effectiveness; and (c) availability of required quantity in time. Competitiveness in products leads to global leadership. To achieve this unique position we require out-of-the-box concepts, creative thinking, an innovative approach and dynamic leadership. Above all, we need strong partnership with a network of industries.

From the very beginning of the JV, we wanted to generate an industry consortium with industries funding for themselves. This being a JV, we could have utilized the large industry base available at Russia. However, this would have defeated the very basic purpose of the JV as all the subsystems would have been produced only in Russia, thereby increasing dependence on it for everything. Therefore, a well-articulated policy had to be evolved to build a missile industry consortium for BrahMos. While forming the JV, the Russians also agreed that the missile should be produced in both countries and together we must build industrial capability to establish common standards, fabrication methods and inspection procedures in order to facilitate interchangeability of systems. This would also facilitate the use of JV products by the armed forces of India as well as Russia.

Thus, at the feasibility study stage, it was decided that the missile was going to be unique and produced in both countries. Moreover, in case of any change in the geopolitical situation, the missile could be produced in the respective country to meet the requirement and also ensure continuous product support. It was a conscious decision to approach industries to become partners to the programme by having them invest in the infrastructure.

At this point, I should first narrate the prevailing scenario of defence production in India. After the 1962 war, India needed production of defence equipment and weapons on large scale and resorted to technology transfers and production under license, necessitating funding of infrastructure in the country. Therefore, the Government formed public sector undertakings and ordnance factories for production of defence equipment. There were no private industries that could come forward to establish facilities to compete with the PSUs. Over the years, private industries started popping up but they continued to lose the battle as the Government gave PSUs preferential treatment in terms of choice as well as price. Gradually, PSUs attained monopoly in industries related to aircraft, electronics, vehicles, shipbuilding, battle tanks and missiles. All the defence orders were placed with them. There was no chance for the private industries to grow.

PSUs went in for transfer of technology and production in the case of major systems like tanks, aircraft, missiles and radars. They had to depend on foreign industries in terms of understanding the process and provision of spares. Over the years, this practice made the PSUs technologically inferior. Adding to this, they became larger and larger with huge manpower, out of proportion with respect to the productivity. The equipments became older and due to lack of modernization these industries suffered technological obsolescence. As the armed forces required modern warfare, foreign vendors started aggressive marketing and this led to heavy import of equipment and weapons.

On the other hand, ISRO, an autonomous organization, started involving private industries and also utilizing the best from PSUs. Space vehicles needed special materials and chemicals, special fabrication technology and electronic systems, which forced them to look for options.

This led to the birth of many private industries. Today, I must say that private industries have grown in stature in infrastructure, technological maturity and efficiency, to be able to undertake design, development and production of major defence equipment. It is time for a rational policy to utilize both public and private sectors in a judicial manner, with the aim of quality production on large scale so that there is no dependence on imports. This also means that the PSUs have to be made more efficient, productive and competitive since they have already invested and are investing huge funds from the Government. Appropriate restructuring is essential for these defence PSUs to perform in order to ensure indigenous production at a higher self-reliance ratio. Moreover, private industries must come forward to set up in-house R&D to support design and development, and also form technology partnerships at the frontline areas with foreign collaborators.

The BrahMos Way

In the IGMDP era, many industries started building up core competencies in production of ferrous and non-ferrous alloys and composite materials, precision fabrication of components and large-sized structures, electronic systems, avionics, sensors, radars, chemicals, cables, connectors, etc., from raw materials stage to systems. The industrial base, therefore, was strong enough for better utilization for the BRAHMOS missile and ground systems. We needed to build around this capability and suggest augmentation of capacities to the industries and make a partnership that would support large-scale production.

Our previous experiences indicated that it would be extremely difficult to give the entire production responsibility to one industry, which would coordinate with all other agencies, integrate the system and deliver to the user. Hence, it was decided to set up our own integration complex and produce all the components and subsystems through an industrial network. The JV did not have funds for setting up facilities at the industries for production of components. Hence, we requested industries to set up a special production facility for subsystems like airframe and requested DRDO to set up the integration complex to be operated by the JV.

PSUs donot invest in building production facilities unless a special provision of funds is made available to them by the Government. Private industries will invest provided there is an assurance of orders; they can amortize the expenditure during production. With this approach in mind, the BrahMos team evolved a policy to retain system design, system engineering, system integration and system management with the company and go for partnerships and MOUs with leading industries for production of subsystems, components and materials. The procedure for implementing this policy is outlined below.

System Design

A group of nearly 50 scientists from DRDO and BrahMos came together at NPOM, Moscow, to interact with the Russian Design Bureaus over the design and interface details based on Indian and Russian process stock technologies. A composite preliminary design evolved which got approval from the joint team. Inputs from multiple DRDO laboratories helped to complete the design process for missiles. RCI designed a high-performance, fast-reaction inertial navigation system, on-board Processors and missile interface units for the missile. The design details on the ground complexes, fire control systems, launchers, mobile command posts and software were developed by DRDO in collaboration with selected industries. The special expertise available with R&DE(E) for design of vehicles and structures helped to configure the shore complex and ship-based installations, leading to patenting some of the concepts and designs. In this process, a design centre came up at BrahMos headquarters with expertise in naval architecture, structures, marine engineering, electrical and electronic systems, gas dynamics, fluid mechanics and transfer alignments. This capability helped in installation of the BRAHMOS system in a number of ships that came for retrofit and others that were being built under new construction programmes.

Another group of scientists undertook the development of simulation packages for war gaming to enable best utilization of the weapon system.

System Engineering

The joint venture became the custodian of the design documents, detailed drawings, process documentation, standards, test methods and reports, inspection and quality procedures, system evaluation and acceptance procedures, flight test plans and test results, and all other relevant documents. The JV also became the focal point for joint reviews and coordination with all design and development agencies.

System Integration

The responsibility of integrating the subsystems as well as assembling the final missile and the mobile complex for land version and the ship complex for naval version has been taken up by the JV. In order to carry out the system integration of the missile, separate facilities have been created with trained manpower and infrastructure at multiple centres. Each technician, supervisor, overseeing engineer and inspector has gone through appropriate training and attestation. All the equipment, tooling, test fixtures and methodologies have also been attested to ensure high quality standards. Each deliverable system has been assured for a minimum of 10 years storage life, requiring meticulous quality control procedures that were evolved jointly by the Indian and Russian scientists with participation of government inspectors authorized by Missile System Quality Assurance Agency (MSQAA). By taking the entire responsibility, the JV resulted in a) complete control of schedule of activities, supply chain management, industry coordination and problem solving to ensure deliveries to the end user on time; and b) quality checks at assembly stage and final checkout.

System Management

The contracts with NPOM, DRDO, industries and all other agencies were carried out meticulously to detail the tasks, milestones and review methodology to ensure common systems and procedures, followed with a single-point contact. Ultimately, the motto is to meet the schedule of deliveries to the armed forces. This was possible only through integrated management. Finally, this helped to build confidence among customers.

PUBLIC–PRIVATE INDUSTRIAL CONSORTIUM

The integration of public–private industry partnership in the production of the BRAHMOS missile was a unique concept. The criteria for the identification of industry partners had been laid out and was carefully reviewed and verified. The criteria for selection of partners was based on (a) their willingness to invest own funds to support or sustain the capacity and also to increase quantity on requirement basis, necessitating a modular approach; (b) their experience in aerospace technology products; (c) their ability to absorb state-of-the-art technology with high level of knowledge competence; and (d) high governance indicators. The joint specialists team from both countries assessed the manufacturing and production capabilities of various industries and shortlisted the ones who could be partners to BrahMos. This report was presented to the board of directors. The board appointed a specialist committee with board members to scan through these industries.

Based on the final list, Government approval was obtained for the consortium of public and private industry partnership. The best part was, the industries came forward, enhanced their infrastructure by funding from their own source, and manufactured subsystems for an advanced supersonic cruise missile. They made exclusive production set-ups for the missile subsystems. There were many other small private industries who either provided support to BrahMos directly or became subcontractors to major industries. In all, 20 major industries and more than 200 small- and medium-scale industries became partners to BrahMos. All these tasks were carried out in record time in a concurrent manner, without knowing the number of units to be produced as there was no production order with us at that point of time. It was amazing to see the overwhelming response of the industries expressing full confidence in the leadership. They were confident that the missile would be produced in large numbers. In many other cases where the industries participated in development, product acceptance by the user took many years; by that time the technology would become obsolete. Finally, only PSUs were given the production orders. In course of time, industries lost interest in participating in the development of defence equipment. This trend was reversed by BrahMos. Human resources comprising more than 20,000 specialists, technicians and engineers have been engaged in the manufacture of BRAHMOS subsystems at different industries. The major industries and the systems/subsystems produced by them are enumerated in the accompanying table. The list is not exhaustive.

Industry	Systems/Subsystems
Larsen & Toubro, Mumbai	Composite airframe, canister, launchers for ships, FCS, missile components
Godrej & Boyce, Mumbai	Metallic airframes (nose cap, wings and fins, CPHS, F3), launcher and launch tubes/containers
HAL, Hyderabad and Korwa	INS
ECIL, Hyderabad	Communication equipment, MCP, MAL integration
Astra Microwaves	Telemetry
Ananth Technologies	OBC, MIU, telemetry
Data Patterns, Chennai	FCS, SCAN seeker, COE, ATE, airborne PCD
BHEL	Launcher systems
BEML, Bangalore	Vehicles for MAL and MCP
HEB, Tiruchirappalli	Batteries
BATL, Thiruvananthapuram	All metallic parts of the missile including airframe and booster; containers, airborne launcher

Integration Facility

Along with the consortium, we simultaneously started establishing the system-integration facility at Hyderabad. Today, it there has become a world-class state-of-the-art complex.

We built another integration complex at Nagpur. This facility was intended to augment the production rate as we had started to receive large orders from the three services. A network of technical positions had been established for storage, maintenance and operations of the delivered systems. A proactive step was taken to establish a unique product support centre close to these facilities for real-time support and to keep the equipments in ready-to-use condition. Today we have state-of-the-art production, integration and storage facilities.

During the initial phase of the partnership, only a limited quantity was ordered for development trials. That enabled us to establish the technological competence of the industries. This was done through appropriate training, visits to Russian industries, involving Russian specialists to contribute in detailed drawings, working for tolerances, infusing new technology areas, developing equivalent materials, attestation of the quality level of technicians to undertake special product realization, involving government inspectors at regular intervals, large-scale qualification tests to prove the subsystems, and so on. Several reviews and interactions have tremendously helped these industries to upgrade themselves, making them committed towards product excellence and the joint venture. The development flight trials of the BRAHMOS went exceedingly well, giving 100 per cent success to the Navy and resulting in placement of production orders by the Indian Navy in 2005. Further, trials of the land-version missile led to the placement of orders by Indian Army in 2006.

PART 7

In the Horizon – The Future

"When an idea exclusively occupies the mind, it is transformed into an actual physical or mental state."

– Swami Vivekananda

BrahMos Aerospace is a growing enterprise and a role model of high repute, heralding the successful cooperation between two great nations. The progressive thinking continues to make the organization vibrant. The BrahMos Vision 2050 is aligned with the organization's credo and will guide us with benchmarks for the coming years.

15

Vision 2050

Beyond Supersonic

The Bible Proverb 29:18 says: "Where there is no vision, the people perish." The same holds true for the survival of any organization in the long run. The organizational growth depends on the foundation it has created for sustained growth. The long-term existence of the organization depends on realization of newer high-performance products and the team behind it. Superiority of products in terms of performance, reliability, cost-effectiveness, longer shelf-life and on-time product support will help maintain the organization's long-term viability. New products certainly bring new dimensions to the organization, thus making it formidable.

At BrahMos,a team comprising young energetic engineers and experienced scholars in various fields have created a vision document called BrahMos Vision 2050. The vision document has been divided into two portions. First is the BRAHMOS with current systems and its newer roles, and the other is BRAHMOS-II. For the current systems, the document covers a series of activities such as augmentation of the facilities for production and deliveries to meet the schedule and construction of new product support facility. There are suggestions of new roles for the existing system, such as an air-launched version, and technological upgrades of subsystems for performance improvements and for undetectability. The document also suggests various upgrades with newer versions, such as a miniaturized BRAHMOS for multiple platforms– aircraft, submarine and ship. The realization of a hypersonic version, the BRAHMOS II, is emphasized to continue being the world leader in cruise missile. Hypersonic technology will be the future in terms of its astonishingly higher speed with reduced cost.

> Hypersonics refer to speed greater than Mach 5, which is about 6,000 km per hour. Theoretically it is possible to reach Mach 25 – 30,000 km per hour – in the hypersonic regime. As speed will be the deciding factor for future space travel and reduction in costs incurred, attempts are being made worldwide to develop technologies for realizing a vehicle that can fly at a hypersonic speed of more than Mach 5 and return as a reusable system. In the book *Thoughts for Change – We Can Do It* authored by Dr Abdul Kalam and myself, we have identified hypersonics as the futuristic core technology for aerospace programme and one of the 10 unique technologies that will rule the world.

Hypersonic Research Centre at IISc

To pool in the best resources in India and to carry out advanced research in hypersonics, a centre of excellence was established at Indian Institute of Science (IISc) in November 2011. The centre has organized an international conference on hypersonics with participation of several countries to debate over the technological challenges required to achieve a reliable hypersonic vehicle.

France is pursuing its French-LEA hypersonic programme; Japan has undertaken the Hytex programme; the USA has got hypersonic vehicles like HyFly, X-43 and X-51. Conceived in 2004, X-51 made its first 'captive carry' flight in December 2009. The next two flight trials of X-51A ended prematurely. The third trial lasted only for 15 seconds and lost control due to faulty control fin. In the next flight on 1 May 2013, the cruiser travelled about 425 km (230 nautical miles) in just over six minutes reaching a peak speed of Mach 5.1.

In India, DRDO is pushing ahead the development of the Hypersonic Technology Demonstrator Vehicle (HSTDV) with an aim to demonstrate autonomous flight of a scramjet-integrated vehicle using aviation turbine fuel. Initially, the hypersonic vehicle would fly at an altitude of 30 km to 35 km at 6.2 to 6.5 M, with flight duration of 20 seconds. To realize this, technologies being developed at DRDL are aero-propulsion-integrated configuration, hypersonic airintake, hot structures, single-expansion ramp nozzle, scramjet combustors, etc. The technologies to be developed for a long-duration flight (~600 sec) are nose tip, wing and tail leading edges, protective coating, active cooling of scramjet engine, endothermic fuel, etc.

BRAHMOS-II

The BRAHMOS-II will be configured with a speed of around Mach 5 to Mach 7 and will be operated by a scramjet engine. The challenge will be developing high-temperature materials to be used in the engine for sustaining long-duration operations and in the leading edges of the vehicle and the control structure interaction. Development of scramjet engine is a formidable technological challenge before us.

Scramjet Engine

The engine of the present BRAHMOS-I missile is ramjet, where the air rams into the combustion chamber and gets compressed by the speed itself and mixes with the atomized spray of the fuel. When ignited, the air expands and rushes out of the nozzle thus propelling the missile at supersonic speeds. After the air enters the engine, its speed is reduced to subsonic regime for combustion.

In a scramjet engine, the combustion of the fuel and air takes place when the air itself is in supersonic speed. This provides enormous speed to the carrier vehicle. While it may seem simple enough, the scramjet engine is very hard to realize, particularly due to the high-temperature combustion process.

A hypersonic flight within the atmosphere will generate terrible drag because of which the airframe of the missile will get immensely heated. These temperatures can be many times greater than the surrounding air. Again, maintaining combustion in the supersonic flow of incoming air itself is an additional challenge, as the fuel injection, mixing and ignition cycle have to be completed within milliseconds after the air has entered the engine.

To keep the combustion rate of the fuel constant and for the missile to have a constant speed, it is necessary that the pressure and temperature in the engine are constant too; else it will not be possible for the missile to manoeuvre.

At DRDL, the development of a scramjet engine is in progress. Ground tests have been conducted for 20 seconds duration and have given good results. Spontaneous ignition and sustained combustion have been achieved under supersonic flow conditions. The engine is capable of reaching a speed corresponding to the speed of the vehicle, which is more than Mach 6. This has been very encouraging. With this, the supersonic combustion has been established. This engine will be used in the hypersonic vehicle and flight-tested. The technology will be used as a process stock of India in the JV.

Guidance System

The available guidance systems will not be suitable for hypersonic speeds as the flight vehicle may have to face tremendous vibrations and aerodynamic heating and shock. While both BRAHMOS-I and BRAHMOS-II have similar missions, their mission profiles will vary in terms of induced restriction in speed of operation.

Advantages of a Hypersonic BRAHMOS

A hypersonic missile definitely has an advantage of speed, as in future wars more defensive systems will be employed against cruise missiles. Hence, there will be a greater need to give less reaction time to the enemy to defend himself. For example, an enemy missile base situated at a distance of 290 km can be destroyed in roughly five minutes by BRAHMOS-I. The hypersonic BRAHMOS-II with a speed of Mach 6 can execute the same mission in around 2.5 minutes, thus minimizing the response time by half.

A Hypersonic Reusable Cruise Missile and the Sudarshan Chakra

The next task will be to develop a reusable version of the hypersonic missile. After this, we will embark on the development of hyperplanes with multiple applications.

My mind goes to a very powerful imagery in Hindu mythology – Lord Vishnu with the Sudarshan Chakra on the index finger of his right hand. Its technological marvels leave me amazed. The Sudarshan Chakra is a disc-like super weapon with 108 serrated edges; it always remains in motion to annihilate the enemy and returns back to its original position. Can we think of realizing such a weapon that can fly at a very fast speed, execute the mission and come back? This would be the hypersonic reusable missile.

The present and the upcoming versions of the missile fly towards the target and destroy the target along with itself. Such weapons are for one-time use. In fact, that is the purpose of any missile in war. The reusable cruise missile, on the other hand, will fly towards its target following a designated trajectory, eject the warhead over the target and then return to its home base. This type of missile will be similar to an unmanned aerial bomber aircraft that drops the bomb over its target and returns to its base. Since the speed of the missile is very high, its lethality is bound to be high. Such a weapon platform will create a new paradigm in warfare without risking the pilot's life.

A typical reusable hypersonic air-launched missile flying at an altitude of 30 km–40 km in cruise mode at Mach 7. The typical mission will be carried out through an air-launched missile at an altitude of 10 km and boosted to Mach 3.5 at 15 km altitude. Kerosene-based dual-mode ramjet propulsion will take it to Mach 5 at an altitude of 23 km. Scramjet propulsion will propel the missile with a cruising speed of Mach 7 to an altitude of 35 km. The missile will deliver the payload at the designated target and will fly back to its destination.

Hyperplane

What is a hyperplane? We have heard about the Space Shuttle of the USA. How can we forget Kalpana Chawla, who along with other crew members died at the re-entry stage of the Space Shuttle? Is that a reusable system? Yes, the Space Shuttle can fly many, many times.

You may be aware that the payload fraction of present-generation expendable launch vehicles does not exceed one per cent or two per cent of the launch weight. Thus, to put one or two tonnes in space requires more than one hundred tonnes of launch weight, most of which – nearly 70 per cent – is oxidizer. Such space transportation systems, with marginal payload fractions, are quite uneconomical for mass transportation and to carry freight and people for missions of Earth, Moon and Mars. Definitely, there is a need for developing reusable launch vehicles, which can bring down the cost of placing payload in orbit from the present US $20,000 per kg to $2,000 per kg and eventually to $200 per kg.

At the International Astronautical Federation in 1988 at Bangalore, the Indian team led by Air Cmde (Retd) Gopalaswamy proposed that the pay load efficiency could be improved to 15 per cent compared to the 8 per cent proposed by the USA, Europe and Japan. The idea is to develop a hyperplane vehicle that can take off from conventional airfields, collect air from the atmosphere on its way up, liquefy it, separate the oxygen and store it on-board for the subsequent flight beyond the atmosphere. It will take off horizontally like a conventional airplane using turbo-ramjet engines that burn air and hydrogen. Upon reaching the cruising altitude, the vehicle will use scramjet air-breathing propulsion to accelerate from Mach 4 to Mach 8. During this cruising phase, an on-board heat-exchange mechanism will collect the hot air from the engine and convert it into liquid oxygen. The liquid oxygen thus collected will be used in the final phase of the flight, at the time when the rocket engine burns the collected liquid oxygen and the carried hydrogen to reach the orbit. The vehicle will be designed to permit at least a hundred re-entries into the atmosphere. When operational, it is expected to be capable of delivering a payload weighing up to 1,000 kg to low Earth orbit. It will then be the cheapest way to deliver material to space.

In the case of the hyperplane, the aim is to achieve a larger payload fraction. The Space Shuttle of the USA with 2,000 tonnes takeoff weight could launch only 30 tonnes in low Earth orbit, giving a payload fraction of 1.5 per cent. India's concept of the hyperplane aims to realize 15 per cent of payload fraction. This increased payload efficiency will considerably reduce the launch cost per mission and will enable multiple missions such as transport, reconnaissance, payload delivery and satellite injection.

On a typical mission, the hyperplane will take off with 100 tonnes weight using fan ramjet engine and then be in scramjet mode for nearly 1,000 seconds, during which it collects the leftover air, cools it and separates it as liquid oxygen. This increases its weight to 166 tonnes; thereafter it flies in rocket engine mode using the liquid oxygen and stored liquid hydrogen to deliver a payload of 16 tonnes. This concept of mass addition in flight is unique and has been conceived by Indian scientists.

Space-Based Solar Power

While fossil fuels like oil and natural gas are depleting rapidly and the available renewable (non-solar) energy sources like wind, biomass and ocean thermal/wave energy are limited to about 100 GW, India is now concentrating on terrestrial solar power with its National Solar Mission targets of 20 GW terrestrial solar power by 2020, 100 GW by 2030, and 200 GW by 2052.

Solar energy harvested in space is now recognizable as an option for a 24x7 source of clean, perennial, abundantly available power. The technology for building and orbiting space solar power stations is complex and technologically and administratively challenging; it may take 10 to 15 years to be comprehensively demonstrated in space and needs international cooperation.

There have been several advances in materials and technologies which have greatly enhanced the commercial attractiveness of harvesting energy from space. Considerable advances have been made in enhancing solar-cell efficiencies, in reducing their weight and costs. It is expected that by 2020 electricity from nanotechnology-based solar cells in commercial production will be competitive with electricity from fossil fuels. However, on ground, solar arrays operate only for six to eight hours in the day and this necessitates the use of SSP systems to meet the base load power demands.

In India, the need for space-based solar power stations was identified way back in 1993 in anticipation of the emerging global energy crisis of the 21st century. Since then, work has been carried out on advanced space transportation system design concepts for affordable space solar power.

PART 8

The Lighthouse

"I was always looking outside myself for strength and confidence, but it comes from within. It is there all the time."

– Anna Freud

The importance of the BrahMos joint venture is that it has given gains beyond boundaries, placing India in the club of technology leadership. In fact, it is a game changer if we can use it for future development and production of defence equipment to achieve our cherished mission of self-reliance.

16

WHAT WE LEARN FROM BRAHMOS

The joint venture has been a win–win partnership for both India and Russia and today it stands as a shining example of international cooperation. The BRAHMOS is indisputably the most potent supersonic cruise missile in the world. Delivering the BRAHMOS land-mobile version to the chief of the army, this is what Dr Kalam, who as the then president of India was also the supreme commander of the armed forces, said, "India has always been the fifth or sixth nation in any major milestone, be it the SLV-3, Agni, or the nuclear tests. I always longed for India to become the first nation to possess the most advanced system in the world. BRAHMOS made India proud by making it the first nation to have a universal operational supersonic cruise missile delivered to its armed forces, thereby demolishing the 'sixth nation syndrome'."

BEING THERE FIRST

India was going through a technology-transfer phase with other countries to produce tanks, aircraft and missiles, and learnt little in the process. This was because the product was not the best in the category and no design documents were shared through license transfer. Moreover, all these technology transfers were given to PSUs, who had limited technological competence to absorb inputs and utilize these in designing new systems. The indigenous development of systems at DRDO also suffered due to the considerable time required for developing newer technologies. Due to the technological gap with developed nations, the efforts we made did not allow us to breakeven. If we really had to make a mark, the product must be the best in the world.

The BrahMos joint venture proved to the world that here was a product that no one had achieved. Through joint design, development, production and induction in the services, the BRAHMOS became a unique product for multiple platforms for multiple missions and for multiple targets.

Sharing of core competence in terms of technology and skill is the basis of formation of a JV. In the case of BrahMos, both partners were equally interested in the project right from the very beginning and this interest never faded away. India had to increase its defence capability through the induction of the most modern system in the fastest possible manner. Russia needed funds flow for continuation of development programmes. They could get bulk orders for the Russian industries through this missile programme, thereby also enabling them to create a corporate culture for managing a consortium of industries. Technologically, they could extend the cruise missile capability for high-precision land attack with way points and supersonic steep dive. Keeping this as the motto, both teams worked with full enthusiasm and conducted the first flight within three years after the commencement of the JV. The reliable design and meticulous manufacturing resulted in consecutive successes that further enhanced the mutual trust and confidence between the partners. Regular technical and managerial interactions gave transparency to the programme, while vigilant governance helped avoid any clash of interests. This was done through debates and brainstorming sessions. Above all, there was compassion for each other's national and institutional interests.

Why Not BrahMos Way?

We followed and still follow a unique way of management to leapfrog to a next higher level. Through this, we have proved many theories. What are they? We have established a brand that BRAHMOS means Quality.

Novel Concept

The international joint venture BrahMos was formed between two like-minded countries with a novel concept of a JV Model which successfully developed a high end weapon system. This broke the conventional buyer-seller relationship and made both the countries happy to accept that this is a shining example of technological cooperation. This model has been replicated between India and Russia again in the case of 'Medium Transport Aircraft' project and advanced 'Fifth Generation Aircraft'.

Both countries invested almost equal funding of $ 300 millions and the JV is now manufacturing products worth billions of dollars. The time when the Russian forces would start buying BRAHMOS and also when the export orders would be carried out, the returns would further shoot up. If the advantages are crystal clear, why not this JV model is further multiplied to reap more benefits and to gain technological advantages.

Initially there were many uncertainties about the joint venture, it being the first of its kind. In course of time, many improbabilities turned out to be possible. Some examples:

a) An international JV with a technologically advanced former superpower
b) A government-owned private company
c) Public–private partnership
d) Fielding a futuristic war-winning weapon in a short span of time

Gains for Both Nations

The BrahMos JV broke the conventional buyer-seller relationship.

BrahMos is the first successful joint venture between India and any other country for the design and development of an advanced weapon system. Both countries have invested funds as share capital and technology accrued over two to three decades of experience as knowledge capital. The venture is managed by both shareholders through the nominated board of directors.

For India and Russia, the gains through the JV are multifaceted. In addition to gains in military capability, the JV has yielded technological, financial and corporate gains.

Strategic Gains

A missile that was almost forgotten amid turmoil was revived and given a new life. The ramjet engine that was developed in Russia was supposed to be left unused due to paucity of funds. Thanks to the JV, the money spent by Russia in developing the engine did not go waste. As for India, it could have simply gone for the purchase of an anti-ship missile. But that would have simply continued the traditional buyer–seller relationship without taking the time-tested friendship to the next higher level.

On the technological front, the missile got a sophisticated INS that led it to be grouped among the extra high-precision weapons. Over time, what was planned to be an anti-ship missile also became a land-attack missile. For the first time, the world saw a supersonic land-attack cruise missile. An air-launched version of the missile is also being developed. It can be used to hit the enemy's assets on land or ships at sea. So, from a scrapped anti-ship missile project we have developed a universal missile that can be launched from land and ship to attack either land assets or ships. A missile that was to serve just one wing of the armed forces is now capable of serving all three. Upon requirement, both Russia and India can procure any desired version of the BRAHMOS for their armed forces.

Technological Gains

India understood Russian design methodologies, GOST standards and test and evaluation procedures. Most importantly, without embarking on design and development of an anti-ship cruise missile, we were able to develop multiple versions. The expertise we gained played a crucial role in solving the know-how and know-why issues when augmenting the missile's capability.

No expertise was available with us for the production of a cruise missile. It is because of this JV project that today India can design and produce a cruise missile.

For India, the JV translated into hands-on experience on several technological fronts: the usage of canister and nose cap, an important feature for the survivability of the missile during underwater launch; a contemporary fire control system, the realization of a quick-reaction INS; a software code for the seeker and guidance system which also included the capability to discriminate the target from a group and precisely hitting it; and a state-of-the-art mobile autonomous launcher.

Through the JV, a huge BrahMos missile industry complex has been established. Today, the airframe, the INS and avionics, the canister, explosives for warhead, the solid propellant, the MAL and MCP, launchers and ship-borne launchers are all manufactured in Indian industries. Apart from these, industries dealing with heavy engineering are now capable of undertaking integration in warships as well. Soon, every component of the missile will be manufactured in India to offer our products at a competitive cost.

Russia has got the Block-II and Block-III supersonic steep-diving cruise missile, which was not in its arsenal earlier.

Financial Gains

A huge sum of money was saved by both India and Russia. From Russia we got investment capital, which was otherwise impossible during those difficult days. Although the required money was arranged from the debt, it was still their money. Most importantly, the money that was supposed to go to Russia was reinvested in the JV. So, without any direct financial commitment at that time, Russia became part of the JV. At the same time, millions of dollars invested by Russia in developing the required technologies had been utilized for the JV project.

The conditions and restrictions that India faced during weapon purchases have been entirely eliminated. If an anti-ship missile with capabilities similar to those of the BRAHMOS were imported, the cost would be at least two times more than what the Indian armed forces are paying today, and that too with conditions. Last but not the least, with no equivalent existing anywhere in the world, one BRAHMOS missile completes the job of two to three subsonic cruise missiles.

Total Solutions Company

In India, the process of defence research and development is complicated and tedious. DRDO is the design and development agency for weapon systems. DRDO develops the system, tests its efficacy, and then proves its capability as required by the user. Then the weapon system is produced by a production agency to which DRDO transfers the manufacturing technology. That production agency may leave the marketing of the weapon system to some other agency. These agencies do not have control over each other. If the user wants a modification to be carried out to enhance the combat potential of the weapon, he has to run between poles to get it done.

A product can succeed only when it is conceived, developed, tested, produced, marketed and supported after sales by a single company. Only an integrated company has the inherent flexibilities to make all adjustments to address unforeseen issues.

Innovation

To achieve things, there should be secret recipes. What are they? Our secrets are simple. A strong long-term practical vision, belief in innovation and following Concurrent Engineering practices. Many innovative practices followed in BrahMos:

- This JV model itself is an innovation, particularly at the right time after Gulf War.
- Going for Supersonic speed regime straightaway is another breakthrough.
- Best of technologies and the expertise harnessed to the fullest advantage to realize a product the most cost-effective manner and at less time.
- While development is in progress, the project was put ahead by going for demonstration launch making the Services to place production order.
- Participation of Indian industries with their investment without any commitment for production

- Conversion of loan repayment money as Russian investment.
- Contracting the developmental works to the share holding entities.
- Universality of the missile for sea and land targets.
- Employment of the missile to attack targets through steep dive.

Concurrent Practices and Continuous Upgradations

Since the product was seen in the horizon as a successful prototype, actions were initiated to establish the production lines. This resulted in building up of necessary infrastructure for mass production. As the orders started to come, we started augmenting the production lines. After a certain number of systems were delivered, we started establishing storage infrastructure for the user. After delivering the product to the user, we went on to establish product support centres. With this approach, we were able to reap the benefits of successfully compressing the time frame.

Taking into account the necessity of continuous product modification and upgrade to always be a market catcher, many versions such as Block-II and Block-III LACM have been developed. The air-launched version is in the final stages of development. Next, the development of BRAHMOS-II will be switched to top gear.

Any successful organization must be like flowing water. Water in the clouds has the sea as its destination. It falls as rain on hilly jungles. The fallen water collects itself from the droplets to form a small stream. Many streams combine to form a big stream and the process continues till a river is formed. The river flows down to the plains with enormous energy, which eventually takes it to the sea. If the river encounters a huge depression on land, it first forms itself into a lake. It keeps on filling that depression to collect energy. Then, one day it overflows the depression to continue its journey. On the way it encounters numerous rocky obstacles. It either goes around the obstacle by taking an alternative path or simply blasts away the obstacle with its enormous energy. It merges with various similar small rivers to become a big river and at the zenith it diversifies into branches, nourishes enormous landmass, and finally reaches the sea.

Retaining Control

Another secret is retaining the control through keeping the core responsibilities with us. What are these? While we outsourced many systems, we kept the system design, system engineering, system integration and system management with ourselves.

Win-Win

To sum up, the gains for the Indian side are: (a) a decisive war-winning weapon with Indian armoury (which otherwise would not have been available); (b) mobilization of Indian industries for producing the state-of-the-art weapon; (c) ensuring continuous product support to the armed forces; (d) best of the technologies available for use in many other projects; (e) saving of huge foreign exchange; and (f) becoming an international player for export.

The gains for the Russian side are: (a) support to defence R&D establishments in their country during the financial crisis that was a fallout of the disintegration of the erstwhile USSR (this helped to control the exodus of Russian specialists and also retained their vital technology know-how); (b) utilization of the equipment for testing; (c) sizeable orders to their industries; (d) continuous interactions and utilization of specialists with newer problems, upgradations and versions; (e) mutual exchange of ideas, review methods and type of equipment with Indian industries; (f) newer areas of work – transforming from anti-ship role to land-attack role, supersonic steep dive, etc.; and (g) continuous sustenance of scientific talent for long duration.

PART 9

Trailblazer

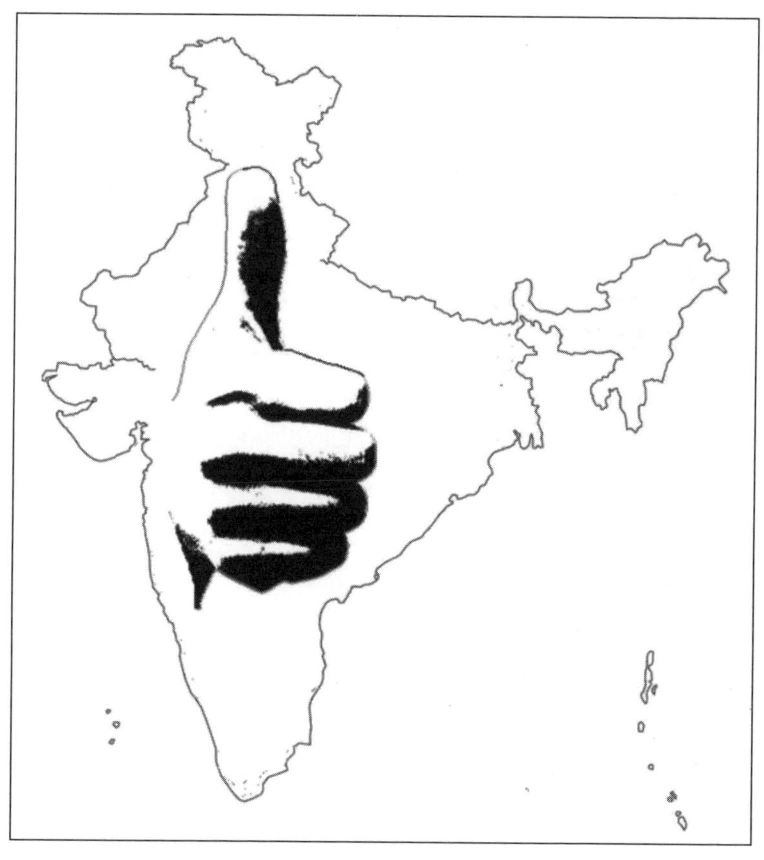

"In modern warfare, a large army is not sufficient; it needs industrial potential behind it.
If the army is the first line of defence, the industry is the second."

– Field Marshal Cariappa

In geopolitics, strength respects strength. A nation will get respect only for its strength. Only a strong nation can advocate peace in the world. The strength of a nation comes from economic prosperity and military power, which in turn comes from technology and knowledge to make state-of-the-art products and systems.

17

Learning from History – Self-Reliance

The ability of man to learn and apply knowledge has been key to his survival. Man is a defenceless animal in the biological world. He does not have talons or teeth like predators, nor does he possess sharp eyesight like eagles. Man has neither acute hearing nor an enhanced sense of smell. A defenceless deer can run away smelling the presence of a tiger. It is said that animals like dogs, cats and elephants have an extra sense to foresee natural calamities like earthquake and tsunami.

That said, the ability of man to 'quickly learn' and produce new gadgets has made him capable to outwit his predators and dominate them into the forests. From where did man learn? He learnt only from the past and the recorded past is nothing but history. It is not that only individuals can learn from their past activities and act prudently to avoid the mishaps of the past; an entire nation can learn from its past and act prudently to prevent committing the same mistake again. A nation that learns from history flourishes and the one that does not, deteriorates. For India, it is the 'need of the hour' to learn from its history, so it can become self-reliant.

India was once a land of prosperity and way ahead of other civilizations. Great emperors like Asoka and Chandra Gupta Maurya ruled and served their subjects with humility. During the reign of Raja Raja CholaI and his son Rajendra CholaI, many South-East Asian countries and Sri Lanka were under the Chola Empire. Though the Indian civilization existed as numerous divided kingdoms, growth, peace and harmony existed everywhere.

This prosperous India became a magic fruit of attraction for many invaders of various races, starting from Alexander, Timur the Lame (Tamer Lang) and Babur to the Europeans, who all looted India's wealth and peace and made Indians their slaves.

In hindsight, we can say that the Indian kings were only watching their enemies coming in hordes with sophisticated weaponry. They themselves did not make efforts to get a superior weapon that would deter invasions. A nation that once upon a time gave scientific thoughts to the whole world lost the wars. We are yet to come out of that 'mindset'.

On the other hand, the nations that enslaved us had a strong industrial base to become economic powerhouses. In economic terms, manufacturing is a very important component for prosperity. Therefore, we Indians must realize that the development of infrastructure and industrial base is vital.

Industrial Revolution

Certain instances like the discovery of fire, the discovery of plants growing from their seeds, and the invention of the wheel were turning points in the history of man's evolution. Some millennia passed after the invention of the wheel without much interesting events. Then came the next revolution – the Industrial Revolution. When the Industrial Revolution started in Europe, many new industries were commissioned. Individuals were encouraged to develop new machines to augment production of trade commodities. This paved the way for research and development efforts to be carried out and feats once considered impossible became possible. In time, machines started replacing human beings in every sphere of production. Not only commodities, even military weapon systems were produced through machines. When arms and ammunitions began to be manufactured through machines, people found that they were able to produce at an unimaginable rate. When wars are fought, the rate at which the fighting forces are supplied with ammunition is a crucial factor. The

European Nations, Russia and America established dedicated military industries just to produce arms and ammunitions. Suddenly, even the small countries realized that they were capable of supporting huge fighting forces and became stronger. Thus, the race to establish, run and maintain military industries began.

Military Industry in the West

By the end of the 18th century, military industries became an integral part of the military capability of a nation. These military industries, research capabilities and contributions from the military became a single entity described as military industrial complex, which became the second line of defence of a nation. General Eisenhower, supreme commander of the Allied Expeditionary Force during WWII and later the US president, first coined the term military industrial complex (MIC). These military industrial complexes produced high-technology weapons of those eras and nations also continuously upgraded their MICs to attain superiority over the enemy.

During WWI, it was found by the fighting sides that their war-waging capability was actually based on their MIC and not much on the strength of their soldiers. After the end of the war, every country in Europe regardless of their political alignment developed their military industry complexes rapidly.

During WWII, Germany suddenly invaded the USSR thus violating a non-aggression pact that existed between them, and almost drove the latter to a point of total annihilation. But the USSR fought back from that miserable situation and defeated Germany. It was a crucial move made by the Soviets in the beginning of the war which fetched them victory. The Soviets knew that their strength was their industrial

> During WWII, approximately 280,000 armoured vehicles (tanks, armoured personnel carriers and other armoured vehicles), 105,000 artillery systems (howitzers, field guns, rocket launchers), 730,000 military aircraft (all sorts of fighter, bomber and transport aircraft), 700 warships (frigates, cruisers, battleships), and 1,500 submarines were collectively produced by the USA, the USSR, the UK and Germany.

might. It was a clear understanding that they could win the war only with their industries. So they embarked on a mammoth transfer of their industries to the Far East, away from the reach of the German bombers. Trains carrying troops to the frontlines were returning with sections of dismantled Soviet industries. It took time for the Soviets to rebuild those dismantled factories deep inside Russia. They started to manufacture the necessary military hardware and supplies. Initially the production was very slow but it slowly picked momentum and later ran on full steam. They supplied their forces with the necessary weapon systems with renewed vigour. The Soviet forces were able to push back German forces and reached Berlin, to hoist their 'hammer and sickle' flag on Reichstag.

It may be recalled that during WWII the first guided missile, V-2, was deployed by the Germans. The famous aerospace scientist Wernher von Braun who developed the V-1 and V-2 rockets showed their performance to Hitler. Amazed by the V-2, Hitler ordered its deployment in the war. He asked von Braun how many he could produce. The scientist politely told him that he would produce 250 missiles in a year's time. Hitler roared, "You will produce 250 missiles per month from next month onwards. You are empowered to use any industry for that purpose." Germany produced 250 V-2 missiles per month and deployed them. This revolutionized the war theatre with the entry of guided missiles and a military industry complex to produce them.

Mankind never saw arms production carried out with this much fury. Just imagine how much steel, coal, diesel, gasoline and manpower would have been used to produce these many weapon systems. All these steel, petroleum and coal industries needed support systems like mining industries and processing and refining industries. Also, imagine the machineries required for these industries, logistics, etc. I have not included the trucks, jeeps and other vehicles that also played a huge role in combat effectiveness.

INDIAN SCENARIO

While we have excellent government-funded public sector units, they alone will not be able to form the military industry complex. Even now, the import content for defence system is more than 60 per cent. If we have to increase the self-reliance index, we have to produce weapons and equipments in large quantity in Indian industries. Therefore, a military industry complex for India should be a consortium of both public and private industries. In the words of KM Cariappa, India's second field marshal, "In modern warfare, a large army is not sufficient; it needs industrial potential behind it. If the army is the first line of defence, the industry is the second."

At BrahMos, we work with 205 partner industries from India and 7 from Russia, thereby creating the 'industry consortium' capable of producing weapons and weapon systems at the required level. BrahMos has set up a wonderful model of industry consortium that can be replicated to bring together both public and private industries to form a military industry complex.

Does any MIC exist in India? The answer is no. There is no organized MIC in India and there are reasons for that. The time during which the Industrial Revolution started, India was under the tight grip of slavery. India was kept away from developments elsewhere, as the British needed raw materials from India for their industries to run. This denial resulted in the limited growth of Indian industrial infrastructure.

After Independence, public sector units were formed for military equipment production. Many private industries have now come to support the indigenous production. However, the non-existence of an MIC in its real form is hurting the nation's self-reliance.

Projected Military Requirements of India

India is the 10th largest economy in the world. Since the economic liberalization of 1991, India's GDP has been growing at a higher rate. In the year 2012–13, the real GDP Growth was around 4.9 percent. According to the Planning Commission's report, the contribution of agriculture was 1.79 per cent, industry 3.12 per cent and Services 6.59 per cent. The decline in manufacturing is alarming and steps are being taken to rectify this. According to the prediction by Euromonitor International, India will be the third largest economy in the 2020s, measured in purchasing power parity (PPP) terms. The country possesses a good amount of skilled human resource potential, with 65 per cent of the population below 35 years of age. India's defence spending was US$ 41.2 billion in 2012 and is expected to grow at a CAGR of 13.08 per cent to reach US$ 67.87 billion by the year 2016, according to ICD Research. India's spending on platforms such as aircraft, tank, ship and radar will be approximately $150 billion in the year 2017 according to McKinsey analysis.

Along with the military sector, the civilian aviation domain too is a lucrative market. It is predicted that the Indian civil aviation market will grow rapidly in the forthcoming years, thus requiring a large number of aircraft. Presently airline operators are sourcing aircraft from abroad as there is no indigenous transport aircraft. If an indigenous aircraft is available to the airline operators, then imagine the level of investments saved from sourcing a similar aircraft from abroad.

In the forthcoming decade, to sustain and augment the present growth India will require enormous energy supplies. It is predicted that India will require about a seven-fold increase in electricity. This requirement can be met only through nuclear power generation. So nuclear power generation is also a lucrative market towards which the Indian MIC can contribute.

How Are We Meeting It?

We are almost self-sufficient in strategic military systems – that is, nuclear-tipped ballistic missiles. But strategic military systems are used only for trial and training purposes. They are just deterrence factors, so nobody uses strategic systems. On the other hand, tactical military systems like tanks, warships, combat aircraft and associated weapons are regularly used to hone the combative skills. These need to be regularly replaced by new systems. For tactical military systems, we are dependent only on imports. Today India is the largest weapon importer. But is importing weapon systems good for a nation?

Problems in Importing Weapon Systems

a) The seller will be the master and India the dependent.
b) The seller country's policies affect India.India may have to support

countries that are against Indian policies because of the persuasion from the seller country.

c) The seller delays and India suffers.The seller may delay the delivery and India has to pay the price both economically and militarily. After delivering the missiles in time, the seller may delay the delivery of spares and support systems.

d) A selling country will never sell a weapon platform that is in service in its own armed force. There will always be an export-quality weapon system. In non-military business an export-quality material is a superior material; in military business it is the opposite. An export-quality weapon system will always be inferior to the ones used by the parent country. If we are buying a military aircraft, critical sensors like radars may be downgraded or associated weapons will be downgraded. No country sells a weapon system superior or equivalent to theirs. Very rare exceptions may exist if the selling country needs funds desperately. But that is very rare!

e) The seller never gives the source code of a critical system's software so that the buyer will not be able to modify the system according to their requirement. The buyer will have to depend on the seller to make the modification, thereby revealing their intentions. Suppose we want to modify a certain radar to detect some type of weapon platform that the seller has sold to another nation. We have to call the seller to modify it and he will then know that we want to detect such and such platform.

f) The cost of life cycle and maintenance may be high. The seller will sell the missile for a cheap price. From the outside, the offer will seem to be a steal.Only later we will realize that the missile has been sold for a cheap price but the support systems are costly beyond expectation. Without the support systems the missile cannot be exploited maximally. So we have to buy those support systems also!

g) In spite of paying a huge amount, during a crisis embargoes may be enforced thus blocking the arterial supply of necessary spares that are required to continue the war effort.

h) The seller country may impose conditionsas part of the end-user agreement.The agreement may even demand that those weapon systems should not be used for offensive purposes.

i) The seller includes delivery charge in the missile's cost.

j) India always depends on the seller for maintenance.Every time the OEM has to be contacted and they will send their engineers to our bases for maintenance.

k) The integration works will be carried at the OEM's place in the case of anti-ship versions. For that, the vessels have to sail to that place. They have to spend time there for getting integrated with the weapon system.

l) Weapon trials will be conducted at the OEM's convenience.

m) Separate charges might be imposed for testing the weapon system.

n) Then the vessel has to sail back to India,spending an enormous quantity of fuel.

o) If a selling country clinches a bulk purchase order, an enormous number of jobs will be generated in that country. For example, if we are buying 10 transport aircraft from a country, some 30,000 jobs will be generated in that country. So, imagine the number of jobs that would result from 45,000,000 crore rupees worth of weapons purchased in the near future. If those purchases are made from India itself, the corresponding jobs will be carried out by Indians for Indian companies. Ultimately, the money spent will circulate within India, thereby improving its economy.

p) There exists a contemporary technology called radio frequency identification (RFID) tag. This tag will emit a radio frequency signal when it receives a particular signal from a checking system. Each RFID tag can be given a unique code to reply. In such a way, these tags are used to track the movement of goods and serve as an important tool in the logistics industry. But those same RFID tags can be installed in the weapon systems sold by the seller. Then by some clandestine means, those RFIDs can be queried and RFIDs will reply. By identifying the geographical location of the reply, the location of the weapon system can be easily found out. Though any such tracking incidents have not been reported, we cannot say that these may not occur!

q) If the seller senses any violation in the usage of the weapon system during a war, there is a possibility that a small part of the weapon system will be turned off by the seller through satellites.

We may also face the following difficult conditions due to importing a weapon system.

Inferior Systems

First and foremost is that a selling nation will never sell a weapon platform that is in service in its own armed force. There will always be an export quality weapon system. In non-military business an export quality material is a superior material whereas in military business it is opposite. An export quality weapon system will always be inferior to the ones used by the parent country. If we are buying a military aircraft, critical sensors like radars may be downgraded or associated weapons will be downgraded. No nation sells a weapon system superior or equivalent to theirs. Very rare exceptions could only exist if the selling nation needs funds desperately. But it is very-very rare!

Sky-high Cost

Any weapon system purchased from a foreign nation comes with a sky-high price tag. The system would be inferior to the one possessed by their military. Even that may be acceptable because no nation would sell a system as capable as their's! They follow Machiavelli's ideas. They would have spent considerable money in developing a system. They intend to retrieve that money by selling inferior systems to the importer and that too in the first lot of order. A sky-high price tag for an inferior system and an advanced system for their military at our expense!

Unacceptable Terms and Conditions

Sometimes the seller nation may impose a condition called as end user agreement. That agreement may even demand that those weapon systems, which are meant for offensive operations should not to be used for offensive purposes. The seller country may even send some of its experts to verify that whether we had used the system for any offensive operations!

Unreliable Support During Crisis

In spite of paying huge amount, during the crisis time embargoes may be enforced thus blocking the arterial supply of necessary spares that are required to continue the war effort. India is no new to such embargoes!

Subversive Tracking

There exists a contemporary technology called Radio Frequency Identification (RFID) tags. This tag will emit a radio frequency signal, when it receives a particular signal from a checking system. Each RFID tag can be given a unique code to reply. In such a way, these tags are used to track the movement of goods and serve as an important tool in the logistics industry. But those same RFID tags can be installed in the weapon systems sold by the seller. Then by some clandestine means, those RFIDs can be queried and RFIDs will reply. By identifying the geographical location of the reply, the location of the weapon system could be easily found out. Though any such tracking incidents have not been reported, just because there are no reports, we cannot say that this may not occur!

Sabotage

Assume that we purchase a weapon system under 'End user' condition. Naturally there may be question that, how will the other nation react if that condition is violated. As in the previous point, they can track the location of that system. If the seller senses a violation then, there is a possibility that a small part of the weapon system could be turned off by the seller nation through satellites at times of war. Though such instances have not occurred but there is no way to deny the existence of such possibility also!

Ever Dependent on the Seller

If the purchased weapon system requires a solution for some teething problem that involves a design level modification then we have to depend on the seller. The seller may even put some conditions such that even if with our ingenuity we introduce the required modification we cannot claim Intellectual Property Rights (IPR) for our modifications!

Delay and Poor after Sales Support

If by chance the seller delays the deliveries we only have to pay the price as reduction in terms of fighting capability! There is every possibility that the seller nation says so many stories for the delay.

Indigenous Customisation Impossible

The seller never gives the source code of a critical system's software so that the buyer may not be able to modify the system according to its requirement. Even for this we have to depend on the seller to make the modification, thereby revealing our intentions. Say if we want to modify certain radar to detect some type of weapon platform that the seller has sold to another nation. We have to call the seller to modify it and he will know that we want to detect such and such platform. If at all we get the source codes for a system then that system will definitely not be a contemporary one!

Bending with the Seller Country

Above all, the seller nation's foreign policies will affect us. We may be required to support the countries that are against Indian policies or oppose countries that are friendly to us because of the persuasion from the seller nation.

Job Creation/loss

Recently a new concept called as 'job creation' has emerged. If a selling nation clinches a bulk purchase order, then that nation will generate enormous number of jobs. For example, if we are buying 10 transport aircraft from a country, then some 30000 jobs will be generated in that country. Then imagine the number of jobs that would result from 45000000 crores worth of weapons purchase in the near future. If those purchases are made from India itself then those jobs will be carried out by Indians for Indian companies. Ultimately, the money spent would circulate within India thereby improving our economy.

Corruption, Aggressive Marketing and External Pressure

Corruption is inherent in an arms deal. This exists not only in India but all over the world this is the trend. But in the Indian perspective it has more weightage. When a weapon system is sourced from abroad usually voices raise stating corruptive practices were carried out.

We even have witnessed a foreign company approaching our judiciary for continuing with a particular tender process of our armed force, since the tender was awarded to an Indian Company. Also aggressive marketing by the seller nations to an extent become too much irksome to bear. The seller nations create an extraordinary politico-diplomatic pressure on us to buy their systems.

Myth of Import

Dr. Siddhartha said, "(a) No country parts with the best product. So what is sold to us is only with second grade technology. (b) Design knowledge is not shared and the product is sold under license, recovering the cost spent on development. (c) The seller country controls through spares and critical inputs and makes us ever depending on them".

Do we need to continue import of weapons and equipment forever? How do we improve our self-reliance ratio? How do we mobilize indigenous talents to produce the best of the products? The remedy is: "Military Industry Complex".

18

MILITARY INDUSTRY COMPLEX

*"It was surprising that whereas every country wanted to produce her own war material, in India, even very senior officials and Ministers wanted to remain dependent on foreign countries and governments for military hardware and would not take any initiative for local production. These people did not understand that a country must not remain forever dependent on another country for her military requirements as, in the event of a war breaking out, that country could stop supplies, putting the receiving country in dire difficulties when her need would be the most acute."**

–Pandit Jawaharlal Nehru

** BN Mullick, "My Years with Nehru 1948-1964" (Allied Publishers, 1972, p. 130)*

Even today, we depend on imports for most of our requirement. There are reasons for such a state of affairs. The first and foremost reason is that developed nations have an industrial set-up that is at least a century old. The long time they had been in business has allowed them to create a strong foundation that aids in further augmenting their products' features or introducing a new product in accordance with trends. When India became independent, only a handful of industries existed within the country. The meagre money available with the Government could not provide for a large industrial infrastructure immediately. Later, public sector undertakings (PSUs) were established by the Government as part of industrial build-up.

Public Sector Undertakings

For nearly every field, the Government established PSUs. For example, in the field of public transport sector, state governments formed public transport companies; for air transport two PSUs were started, Air India and Indian Airlines. For aircraft manufacturing Hindustan Aeronautics Ltd (HAL) was established. For petroleum exploration and related activities, Oil and Natural Gas Corporation (ONGC) was started. For selling oil and gas products, there were Hindustan Petroleum Corporation Limited (HPCL) and Indian Oil Corporation Limited (IOCL). For steel manufacturing, Steel Authority of India Limited (SAIL) came into existence. Like these, today there are around 250 companies in India covering almost every commercial sector and under the direction of a ministry dealing with that sector. In the beginning they were essential as there were no other alternatives.

Ordinance factories and defence PSUs like HAL, BEL, BEML, BDL, MDL, GRSE, GSL and HSL have monopolies to produce their respective products under license. However, capabilities being limited, the import content is large. It is an open secret that the PSUs will never be in a position to deliver the desired output and constitute the military industry complex. So, what is the remedy?

Developing a Defence Industry

Realization of any advanced technology product involves stages like research, development, technology transfer absorption and production of systems with performance, quality and cost-effectiveness. There are three routes to realize this.

Route A (know-how) is obtaining the licensed technology with fabrication drawings and the production process supplied by the foreign manufacturer. The concerned industry will realize the product but in this process industries achieve only limited know-how with high life-cycle cost. Industrial growth happens only in low-technology areas. What we have achieved was creation of large infrastructure, manpower and focussing on the weapon delivery to the user. We lost the indigenous design capability. Moreover, we have to depend on the foreign manufacturer for the spare parts. This approach will not result in acquiring the desired technology from any angle and will only widen the technology gap.

Route B (know-why) begins with the design and development being done indigenously and the production process done within the country. Industries acquire not only 'know-how' but also 'know-why' with low life-cycle cost. Here, critical technologies are realized and many main and allied industries in high-technology areas grow. The main hurdle is the time and cost overrun.

Route C entails indigenous research and development with limited collaboration in the realization of critical technologies. Indigenous R&D dominates this option. In this process, the development effort and cost is shared by the collaborators enabling fastest realization of the product with state-of-the-art technology, resulting in global competitiveness.

Product Quality and Value with Design

The design plays a vital role in establishing product quality. Design dictates quality, reliability, produceability and cost. Design, in turn, is powered by knowledge content.

Competitiveness

Technological competitiveness can be achieved through highly competitive products. The dimensions of competitiveness are product excellence, cost-effectiveness and delivery on time.

Concurrent engineering practices were used in the development of the Prithvi surface-to-surface missile. There were about 200 technological packages, out of which 20 were critical. Various subsystems were identified for the development of the missile and the design and development of these subsystems started at the various work centres simultaneously. The production agencies (PAs) were identified for each of the subsystems. One of the PAs was made responsible for the overall integration of the missile. Design of the various subsystems was reviewed at various levels. Critical design review of these systems was carried out with experts drawn from design and production agencies and academic institutes. Based on the recommendations of the critical design review committee, necessary design modifications were carried out by the production agency. The user was involved right from the very beginning of the design inception. Various subsystems were assembled at the integration centre. The missile was integrated and subjected to user trials. On completion of rigorous trials, the missile was accepted for induction into the armed forces. With adaptation of concurrent engineering philosophy, we were able to save five years in developmental efforts.

When we started development of the medium-range surface-to-air missile Akash, two important technologies dictated the development time. One was the solid propellant-based ramjet propulsion and the other was a command guidance integrated with phased array radar to achieve multi-target tracking and guidance capability. This meant that the ground radar needed to lock on to multiple targets and guide multiple missiles towards intercepting those targets using electronic switching of the beams. Design and development of the radar system was entrusted to a DRDO laboratory. This radar has multiple arrays, each array with several thousands of ferrite phase shifters at different frequencies. The radar beams are steered and controlled electronically in space by programming the phase shifters through computer-controlled logic. Only two countries in the world possessed the required technology and it was fully guarded. No expertise was available in India either in design and development or for production of the system.

Design and development of the phase shifters was entrusted to Indian Institute of Technology (IIT), Delhi, because in the entire country Professor Bharti Bhatt and Professor Kaul were the only two academicians who knew about phase shifters. Solid State Physics Laboratory, another DRDO laboratory, helped in development of speciality material, and CEL, a public sector undertaking, assisted in the production on receiving technology transfer from IIT. The empowerment of the institution to develop the new technology was accomplished through continuous reviews and help from the R&D labs and concurrent productionization support by an industry.

This resulted in the development and establishment of technology in a short period of three years. Production commenced from the fourth year.

Graduation of Indian industry

In the early 60s, through technology transfer, industries got process for fabrication, equipment and training for the manufacture of the system. But with DRDO initiated programmes, like sonar, EW and IGMDP, the industries slowly graduated to the level of evolving and manufacturing. During 90s, industries attained the stage of build to design, i.e., the design by the DRDO, Indian industries were able to develop systems, such as, light combat aircraft. In another decade, industries grew to the stage of build and design with the capability to build to specification. Thus, a matured defence industry base with both public and private was formed thus becoming a strategic partner to R&D.

The BrahMos Way

In the IGMDP era, many industries started building up core competencies in production of ferrous and non-ferrous alloys and composite materials, precision fabrication of components and large sized structures, electronic systems, avionics, sensors, radars, chemicals, cables, connectors, etc., from raw materials stage to systems. The industrial base therefore was strong enough for better utilization in the realization of BRAHMOS missile and ground systems. We needed to build around the capability and suggest augmentation of capacities of these industries and make such partnership which infuses such a confidence in them that they would be partners during large scale production.

Through our past experiences we were aware that it would be extremely difficult to give the total production responsibility to one industry, which can coordinate with all other agencies, integrate the system and deliver to the user. Hence, it was decided to set up our own integration complex and produce all the components and subsystems through industrial network. JV was not provided with funds for setting up facilities at the industries for production components level. Hence, we resorted to an approach of requesting industries to set up special production facility for subsystems like airframe and requesting DRDO to set up the integration complex to be operated by the JV. Moreover, being a joint effort between the two countries, considerable amount of coordination was required to put things together to ensure timely delivery of quality systems to the users.

BRAHMOS FORMULA

- Robust Design with unique world class capabilities (Best in the World)
- Systematic validation of systems, Simulation, Checkout procedures and reviews establishing reliability at every stage of development
- Incorporating the lessons learnt through earlier experiences of Prithvi and Agni, and thinking a step better in the product performance
- Continuous performance improvements, upgradations and new versions for Customer delight, utilizing the experts from India & Russia
- Strong customer loyalty to the Brand
- Consortium of industry partners keeping design, integration and management with JV. All stakeholders networked with integrated management system and transparency in operation
- Faster execution of the tasks due to autonomous operation of JV & empowerment
- Utilization of young energetic talent force with Pride in working for world-class missile for the nation

Shaping the Procurement Policy towards Self-Reliance

The Government of India has shaped up the procurement policy in its Defence Procurement Policy (DPP) 2013. The main objective of DPP-2013 is to increase the indigenous content by giving a boost to Indian defence industries, both public and private. Capital acquisitions are of three types: a) buy, b) buy and make (India), and c) make. Buy means outright purchase of an equipment. It emphasizes a minimum of 30 per cent indigenous content on cost basis. The offset helped the participation of a large number of medium-scale industries. Acquisitions covered under buy and make (India) cover systems developed by a foreign industry and technology provided for production by Indian industry. This must have a minimum 50 per cent indigenous content on cost basis. Acquisitions covered under make (India) will include production of strategic, complex and security-sensitive systems (no possibility of import); systems designed, developed and produced indigenously (DRDO + industry or consortium of industries or one industry); and systems jointly designed, developed and produced under JV (for example, BrahMos). There is a minimum of 30 per cent indigenous content on cost basis. The thrust given on the offset policy with increased indigenous content for production of systems will increase the participation of more number of Indian industries in the national development.

Present Ambience and Requirements

An important factor prevailing in the present context is the absence of coherence and discrete relationship between the stakeholders viz. Government; Armed Forces; R&D Organizations and the Industries. This resulted in the large import of weapons and equipment due to which there has been continuous dependence on other countries for spares / equipment; there is no effective coordination between R&D organization and Industry as a single entity; and absence of "Mind to Market" thinking.

There are both advantages and disadvantages in all these four sectors of stakeholders. Identifying the bottleneck areas and resolving them and by unifying the strengths of the stakeholders will bring synergy in developing products in the niche areas of technology. Let me narrate the strengths and weaknesses of the stakeholders in the succeeding paragraphs:

Government has got progressively improved Defence Procurement Policy to boost the indigenous production of systems and equipment. Moreover, the offset policy guidelines outlined will induce active participation of industries in the development of systems. More on the benefits of the procurement policy is outlined in the earlier paragraph. What Government can do further is that the thrust should be given on the Long term Defence Strategy and Vision for Defence Industry growth, involving large number of Private Industries as production partners. Government should open up the access for renowned global Companies for having partnership with Indian industries to result in the flow of new manufacturing techniques and state-of-the-art technologies to share with our industries. This will in turn result in the realization of high quality technology products. Allocation of more funding by Government for R&D & infrastructure for establishment and nurturing of advanced research labs and Foundries will strengthen our indigenous R&D capability to help the industries. As in many countries, Legal provision for "Use only Indigenous Weapons" will definitely necessitate the indigenous industry growth and their investment in R&D and go for JVs in high technology products. Defence PSUs, OFs and major identified private industries should become a single entity.

Our highly committed Armed Forces need contemporary, state-of-the-art weapon system to fight against the enemy in the process of protecting the nation. No country gives the best of the weapon and equipment to other countries. When it comes to the development of system indigenously using home grown technologies, there must be level playing acceptance procedures for these systems. At the time of formulation of Qualitative Requirements (QR), user takes the requirements from the existing best systems and adds tough specification to that. The QR once formulated should be the final and there should not be any change in the midway. This will definitely affect the schedule since change in QR affects the entire chain right from the design to process to production to validation. The change in the trained manpower affects the usage of system by the Armed Forces personnel. In the case of BrahMos, the Armed Forces have raised a separate regiment for the BRAHMOS. Trainings are imparted to the crew at different levels to familiarise with the system and ease of operation. Frequent change of personnel will result in the delay in operation and extended man efforts in providing training to them.

DRDO has got the best brains that puts in all-out efforts to succeed in various missions and development of defence systems. In these five decades, started with the basic research, today, DRDO is capable of building bigger systems and has attained the technological maturity. So far, Rs.170,000 Crs. worth of defence products have been produced and delivered to our users. DRDO has got an excellent track record with success in focussed mission mode projects. As the technologies become obsolescent, fast and proactive adaptations are required to sustain in the rapidly changing technology environment. Technology denial regimes added to the problem of restricting in-flow of technologies. With limited resources and manpower and many projects on hand caused non completion of projects in time. Procedures should not become hindrance to the completion of the projects within time. Judicial allocation of resources to multiple projects will resolve the problem. Giving thrust on Quality of Technology transfer documentation and productionization aspects will accelerate the smooth transfer of technology to the industries.

Large industrial infrastructure is available with Indian Defence PSUs for specific product lines to support Armed Forces (Su-30MKI, T-90S, Radars, Missiles and Ships). At the time of establishment, the main motive was to produce defence systems to cater to the immediate requirement, looking for technology inflow from outside. This has resulted in technology know-how and not the technology know-why due to low absorption of technologies. Low R&D effort in the industries has further worsened the situation. Technological obsolescence and the non-upgradation of machineries suiting to the modern manufacturing techniques led to low productivity and quantity production which has resulted in the high cost for products. Moreover, dire requirement of equipment and systems for Armed Forces forced them to go for import due to the exorbitant delay in delivering the products by the industries. There is tremendous growth with the big business houses by the private players. What is required is the fast absorption of Technologies and increased level of R&D effort. Participation of more Private Players through attractive policies ensures competitiveness.

Military Industry Complex that connects all these stakeholders to take the best out of all is the requirement of today.

Need of the Hour – Military Industry Complex

The need of the Hour is to establish a Military Industry Complex (MIC) at the national level enlisting large and medium industries to be the partners along with Defence PSUs as members of MIC. Procedures are to be formulated which will enable participation of cluster of industries to respond to RFP to design, develop and produce the systems (Irrespective of Private or Public). More thrust has to be given for Government funding for R&D even to Private companies to strengthen the indigenous R&D capability. Regulations and control procedures like USA are to be implemented in managing the private industries for manufacturing of defence systems. Creation of an MIC Authority helps to oversee building up production capability and capacity within India. Encouraging high technology tie-ups / JVs between Indian and other global defence industries will achieve not only competitiveness but also envisage the product for export. India cannot afford to lose any more time in pondering the issue. Indian Military Industry Complex with MIC Authority as regulatory body is an absolute necessity.

This will change the perception of the world towards India from an Importer Country to an Exporting Giant.

PART 10

Reaching the Destination

"Always remember that your present situation is not your final destination. The best is yet to come."

– Anonymous

Right from the beginning of a voyage until its destination, many hurdles – known and unknown –can come on the way. It is the captain commanding the ship who takes the responsibility to make it a safe journey. Likewise, the creation of any organization and its journey to success is the responsibility of the leader and the team nurtured by him. The voyage continues to further missions…

19

A Word from the Captain

During one of my visits to NPOMashinostroyenia, I was surprised to see this particular picture in the rooms of deputy directors-general and other key managers. It was my portrait as a captain standing on the ship called BrahMos. In my humble capacity, I have always considered myself as a team member and a bridge between the Indian and Russian scientists in getting things done based on mutual understandings and discussions at every stage.

On asking them why the picture was displayed prominently, they replied thus: "Everyone at NPOM is grateful to you and this picture reflects that spirit. We are working for a great mission and we respect you." I realized that utmost honesty of purpose and goal clarity had motivated our teams in India and Russia to give their best. How can constant motivation of teams be attained?

Talent Pool

The management of talent and continuous motivation to perform go together. The best talent pool is made up of toppers at universities who aspire to go abroad for higher studies. It is worth all the effort to encourage the talent pool to work within the country, we can achieve the most important requirement of youth power to remain long to carry forward the task. This has been done exceedingly well at BrahMos to keep the best of manpower as the talent pool with an average age less than 30. There,

20 to 25 top students from institutions of national repute are absorbed annually through campus recruitment. They are given six months training which includes orientation programme, visits to Laboratories and Industries to acquaint with the recent developments of the Project. They are given independent responsibility for developing a futuristic system. The place becomes ideal for them to utilize their innovation and creativity. Some 10 years down the line, this precious human resource becomes a part of management and takes the project to newer heights. This is a remarkable success mantra for BrahMos.

Creating Centres of Excellence

Researches in the academic institutions have always been a support for design and development. Academic institutions are a rich source of knowledge and it is necessary to associate the research component with R&D. I have already explained the invaluable contributions of academic institutions. One such example was the successful development of the phased array radar and its indigenous production in India. Many institutions had been involved in development of critical technologies. Keeping in mind the excellent contributions of the academia, we have created centres of excellence to undertake studies related to the futuristic technologies involved in development of advanced weapons. The strength of the Academic institution is identified and based on that Centre of Excellence is established to develop critical technologies that are needed for the realization of technologically advanced products. They become the partner in the development.

Partnership Forums

Be it individuals or industries, recognition is vital for growth and motivation. Forums are platforms for partners to express and share their views and allow them to take ownership in the project.

On 19 February 2013, BrahMos organized Ardhik Diwas (Partnership Day) celebrating 15 glorious years of friendship, trust and achievements since the signing of the Inter-Governmental Agreement for the joint venture. On this occasion, all who had contributed in the formation and growth of the joint venture were felicitated.

On 30 July 2013, an industry meet was organized at Hyderabad to highlight the vital contributions made by public and private industries in making the BRAHMOS missile a world-class and formidable weapon system. It was an occasion to recognize the contributions of 205 Indian industries and 7 Russian industries who are associated with the project. The dedication showed by the industries towards delivering high-quality systems/subsystems is commendable. The grand event was graced by the former president of India Dr APJ Abdul Kalam, who described the BrahMos JV as a fine example of courage and excellent leadership.

Steering Committees with the Customer

Separate steering committees were constituted for Indian Navy and Indian Army. These committees are chaired by the respective vice chiefs, members from the armed forces and BrahMos. Periodical reviews were undertaken to bridge the gap between the developer and the user. The decisions required from the user side were raised and clearances obtained at the highest level. This helped the developer and R&D organizations to understand the system requirement. Some of the activities like installation of launcher and associated systems required extensive participation of the Indian Navy. Interventions and decision making at the highest level helped the project to accelerate.

Enterprise Resource Planning

For greater operational efficiency, there is a need for rationalizing the business processes. Automation and seamless integration of the current processes is an absolute requirement to obtain efficiency. Enterprise resource planning (ERP) is a software tool that helps an organization to manage the business processes including product planning and development, manufacturing and inventory management. It is an integrated system that operates in near real time with a common database supporting all applications. The advantages of ERP are many. It greatly improves the quality and efficiency through smooth running of internal business process resulting in more productivity and thereby leading to better customer satisfaction. It enhances the organization's business by allowing the top management to make critical decisions. We at BrahMos have implemented an ERP solution that brought a big change, majorly in areas like production and product support. BrahMos always stands for the timely delivery of the system to its users.

KEY STRATEGIC ISSUES

Some of the key strategic issues in managing a joint venture are:

- Creating and sharing enough value for the partners, maintaining the win–win strategy
- Maintaining enough strategic consistency and compatibility between the partners
- Containing the complexity of managing vital issues with the joint leadership
- Establishing a sequence of partnership related to credibility, criticality, speed of growth, marketing the product

For successful JV and partnership, these four ingredients are necessary: (a) the ability to maintain faith in each other; (b) the ability to express disagreements with each other in a constructive way; (c) the ability to put the teams together; and (d) the ability to bring each other to account if they are appearing short.

Every milestone we crossed was alitmus test and as a team we converted the problems into challenges and successes. Management practices demand 3Cs – communication, commitment and coordination. Results take centre stage in mobilizing the motivated team rather than hierarchical command and control. After all, it is the delivery that counts in management and leadership. The most important points to note are: (a) visible focus on results; (b) work plans and responsibilities to achieve; (c) constant review and problem solving; (d) tuning the organization structure to meet the defined tasks; (e) networking with partners to outsource more; (f) total control on system design, system engineering, system integration and system management; (g) encouraging employee-development activities with good HR management; (h) instituting appropriate performance-measurement system; and above all (i) expression of courage in decision making.

Constant product upgrade and the birth of new versions with increased capabilities help in maintaining the competitive edge and superiority in the market. Our persistence has always motivated us to keep going even after setbacks and has immensely contributed in converting infinite roadblocks into opportunities. The daring concept of leapfrogging, unique visionary thinking and strategic leadership with determination to get things done have made the joint venture an unprecedented success.

Dr Abdul Kalam has always encouraged students: have a great aim, work hard, acquire knowledge, and inculcate such perseverance that empowers you to overcome the challenges. This advice suits any organization equally well.

When I was in Harvard Business School, Sam Walton gave a lecture. He said: "Commit to your business, believe in it more than anybody else, put deep thoughts in it, live in it and overcome the shortcomings by sheer passion." Because of risks in decisions, entrepreneurship is not for the faint of heart. Cowards do not become good leaders. One has to be bold enough to take risks.

Conclusion

People relying on news programmes and newspapers for updating their IQ may not be aware of such experiences. They may never know the amount of pain, sacrifice and dejection faced and suffered by mission teams working in our research establishments. People generally comment: "Why are these research organizations not delivering anything? They are wasting the money we pay as tax." I want to reiterate that our scientists and defence personnel are not inferior to anybody. They are putting in their best efforts. One purpose of the book is to highlight the sacrifices and rejoices that lie hidden from the limelight. We were plundered by barbaric invasions; our wealth was eroded and kept as exhibits in museums; our traditional education systems were uprooted; we were purposely kept away from the Industrial Revolution; our country was meticulously divided by the colonial rule before it left. But we are regrouping; a new generation is ready; and I see a strong and self-reliant India in the horizon.

இடும்பைக் கிடும்பைப் படுப்பர் இடும்பைக்
கிடும்பை படாஅ தவர்

Successful leaders can never be defeated by problems.
They become master of the situation and defeat the problems.

Words of Wisdom

India is a great nation - A powerhouse of knowledge. We all belong to a great gene of civilisational heritage. India's requirements are large and are steadily growing. To meet out these requirements, to become a global leader and to be among the top three countries, we need organizations and industries that are of world class. We must take on and grow further from this strongly created foundation. Young scientists and technological community must take on to make India stronger and stronger. Nothing is impossible.

So every youth of India must keep this in mind,

**"If we are expected to Achieve Results never before Accomplished,
We must employ Methods never before Attempted,
But with utmost honesty."**

–A Sivathanu Pillai

EPILOGUE

Product competitiveness is a very important aspect in the globalized market. The competitiveness depends on three important factors: (i) product excellence, (ii) cost–effectiveness, and (iii) availability in required quantity and product delivery on time. If we have to ensure the customer's delight, these three aspects are essential.

Product excellence means performance, quality, reliability, newer technologies, and quality procedures and certification. In cost-effectiveness, we look at continuous improvement in product effectiveness, effective life-cycle management, value engineering and cost-control measures. Availability on time is very important. If the system is not available as per the requirement of the user, then whatever effort we have put in is not going to be fruitful. Timely availability requires production infrastructure, trained manpower, contractor management, enterprise resource planning and supply chain management. All of these have to be planned during the initial stage of the programme.

There are various options for realizing a product.

Route A is through technology transfer. For example, in the case of MiG-21, we have gone through license production but with limited know-how and knowledge acquisition. It has resulted in repeating the production in India using kits of parts and we have to still depend on spares from other countries.

Route B is totally indigenous. This also we attempted through Prithvi and Agni. Here we are aware of the know-how and know-why, but the time taken to develop all the technology packages is long.

Route C is technological collaboration in selected areas with the right partner. Here we undertake indigenous R&D and develop an indigenous system, and where we face difficulty we go for limited collaboration with an advanced technology contributor. This is what we tried at BrahMos.

Route C, the third option, is the way to realize the best of the product at the earliest, provided the partnership is perfect and managed well. The advantages are:

- Less cost for development of new product because of sharing the technology stock and fund contribution from each of the countries
- Unique performance characteristics of the new product
- Minimum failures due to constant questioning and improvement at every stage
- Overall reduction in realization time of the deliverable product

At BrahMos, we had to face many challenges because of our diverse cultures, languages, expectations and methods of working, along with different standards for inspection. Through these challenges, though, we always looked at maintaining a win–win situation. In the end, the JV brought us many opportunities including a long-standing strategic partnership, core competence in critical technology and international acknowledgement. The BrahMos became an international product and opened up export possibilities.

The JV management is very important and the structure we have adopted is unique. We have got a board with 6 directors – 3 members are from Russia and 3 are from India. Above the board of directors is a supervisory council founded by the two governments. The BrahMos JV has its own procedure, policies, rules, etc., to enable 'performance'. There is both flexibility and control, and that's how we have configured this JV.

Industries have been our partners throughout the journey. This JV company has not made any investment anywhere. All investments have been made by industries. Today, they are reaping the benefits of it. At present, we are increasing our production capacity because our orders are quite large and exports are also knocking on our doors. However, at this point we are giving priority to our own armed forces. The Government of

India is also coming forward with funding to enlarge the production facilities for supporting the programme. Similarly, the Government of the Russian Federation has given funds for enlarging the production facilities in Russian industries. We are working hand-in-hand. There is no gap, and transparency is totally maintained between the two partners.

At every level we have maintained the participation of the user, which includes industry partners and other inspection agencies. Every partner completely becomes part of the system. This is the only project where the inspection agency confirms before the launch the 100 per cent reliability of the missile hitting the target. This is a major factor that has driven this programme.

Throughout the world, there is no answer to the BrahMos system, even after 12 years of the first launch in June 2001. It is a globally competitive product that tops in speed, precision and power. It proves that a joint venture helps in realizing an advanced technology product in a cost-effective manner, produced in the shortest possible time. Strong commitment from both countries, joint funding, fairness in partnership, shared vision, a high level of commitment, a pool of experts available on demand, mutual learning leading to better performance, access to cutting-edge technology and long-term mutual cooperation are the contributing factors in the success of BrahMos.

From India's point of view, the country's defence potential has increased: it has the most cost-effective supersonic cruise missile straightaway in the armed forces; the availability of process stock products and documentations; and new technological inputs. For Russia, the JV has meant funds flow and continuation of development activities; continuous bulk orders for Russian industries from India; and technological gains with diverse capabilities. Both the countries have gained significantly through the joint venture.

About the Author

Well-known defence technologist and the Architect of the World's best cruise missile BRAHMOS, ***Dr. Apathukatha Sivathanu Pillai*** has more than four decades of rich experience in India's Launch Vehicle and Missile Programmes at ISRO and DRDO. He is fortunate to work with the great visionary leaders who shaped India's Aerospace Programme – Dr. Vikram Sarabhai, Prof. Satish Dhawan and Dr. APJ Abdul Kalam and that made him a Technology Leader in Aerospace Systems. His experiences in multi-project environment and networking skills of R&D Laboratories, Industry and Academia have paved way for the realisation of critical technologies which resulted in the successful development of many systems – missiles, underwater sensors etc. and resulted in the evolution of a successful unique venture BrahMos. Brand BRAHMOS has been successfully inducted in the Indian Armed Forces, as a major strike weapon. He has authored many books including those co-authored with Dr. APJ Abdul Kalam. Many academic institutions in India and abroad have recognised his scientific contributions and awarded Doctor of Science (Honoris Causa). He has number of prestigious awards to his credit which include Padma Shri and Padma Bhushan from the Government of India and Order of Friendship from the Government of Russian Federation.